Volume II
Dinosaurs Past and Present
An exhibition and symposium
organized by the
Natural History Museum
of Los Angeles County

Volume II

Dinosaurs
Past and Present

Edited by
Sylvia J. Czerkas *and* Everett C. Olson

NATURAL HISTORY MUSEUM OF LOS ANGELES COUNTY
in association with
UNIVERSITY OF WASHINGTON PRESS
Seattle and London

Natural History Museum of Los Angeles County
Los Angeles, California 90007

LC87-060944

ISBN 0–938644–23–8 (softcover)
ISBN 0–295–96570–3 (hardcover)

Distributed by
The University of Washington Press
P.O. Box C50096
Seattle, WA 98145-5096

Cover: "Cool Weather" by William Stout. Checklist 116.

Pages i–iii: "Crossing the Flats" by Mark Hallett.
© 1986 Mark Hallett. Checklist 140.

Pages vi–vii: Study for Jurassic Mural by Eleanor Kish.
Checklist 46.

OPPOSITE: *Stegosaurus* by Charles Knight, 1901.
Courtesy American Museum of Natural History.

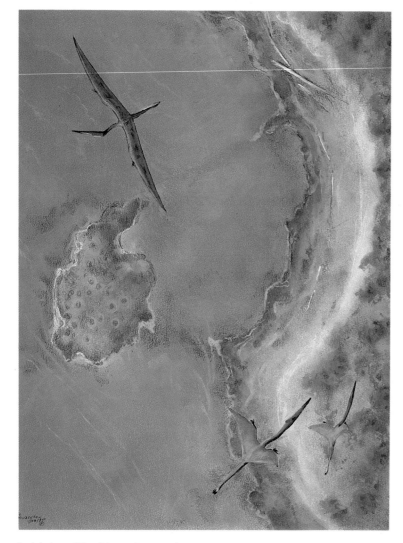

Aerial view of Egg Mountain, a nesting site in western Montana. Pastel by Doug Henderson.

Adult and half-grown hypsilophodonts moving away from a nesting site in western Montana. Pastel by Doug Henderson.

THE
SYMPOSIUM

Natural History Museum of Los Angeles County
February 15, 1986

THE CONTRIBUTORS

Robert T. Bakker, Ph.D. (VOLUME I), holds the Jacob Wortman Curatorship of Fossil Mammals and an Adjunct Curatorship at the University Museum, University of Colorado at Boulder. He began his studies of dinosaurs as an undergraduate at Yale University in the 1960s and continued at Harvard Graduate School where he was elected to the elite Society of Fellows. Dr. Bakker is a skilled artist as well as a dynamic speaker and writer; his recent book, *The Dinosaur Heresies* (William Morrow and Company, Inc., 1986), tells the story of dinosaur evolution in a lively style.

George Callison, Ph.D. (VOLUME I), is especially interested in how fossil reptiles and mammals work. He has led many expeditions to mid-Mesozoic fossil localities of the Rocky Mountains, where his parties have found the smallest adult dinosaurs as well as numerous new and unusual species of other small vertebrates that shared living space with dinosaurian behemoths. Dr. Callison is Professor of Biology at California State University, Long Beach, and Research Associate in Vertebrate Paleontology at the Natural History Museum of Los Angeles County.

Philip J. Currie, Ph.D. (VOLUME II), is Assistant Director, Collections and Research Programmes, of the Tyrrell Museum of Palaeontology in Drumheller, Alberta; he was a major figure behind the development of this new museum and the associated field station, which are together the largest exhibition and research center for dinosaurs in North America. Dr. Currie studied at McGill University, receiving his M.Sc. in 1975 and his Ph.D. in 1982. His major finds have been an *Albertosaurus* skeleton and the earliest known bird footprints. His current research focuses on small theropods, the origin of birds, and ceratopsian behavior. He is Alberta Coordinator of Canada-China Dinosaur Project and Adjunct Professor at the University of Calgary.

Stephen A. Czerkas (VOLUME II) is a professional paleontologist and artist who produces miniature and life-sized models of Mesozoic reptiles that are scientifically accurate and beautifully realistic. His series of life-sized *Maiasaura* babies are on display in the new dinosaur hall of the Philadelphia Academy of Natural Sciences, and his 22-foot (6.7-meter) *Allosaurus* will be on permanent display at the Natural History Museum of Los Angeles County when it returns from its tour with the exhibit Dinosaurs Past and Present. He is currently completing three life-sized *Deinonychus* individuals for the California Academy of Sciences in San Francisco.

Sylvia J. Czerkas, Guest Curator of Dinosaurs Past and Present and coeditor of this book, is a professional artist whose work has been shown in galleries and museums throughout America. She was guest curator and exhibits coordinator for Death of the Dinosaurs at the Griffith Park Observatory planetarium and a continuing series of museum exhibits presented in conjunction with the book *Dinosaurs, mammoths and cavemen: The art of Charles R. Knight* (Dutton, New York, 1982), which she coauthored with Donald F. Glut; she was also Guest Curator for Chevron of a section of the California Academy of Sciences 1985 Dino Fest. With her husband, Stephen, she spends part of each summer digging for dinosaurs.

David D. Gillette, Ph.D. (VOLUME I), has been Curator of Paleontology at the newly opened New Mexico Museum of Natural History in Albuquerque for the past four years. Since moving to New Mexico, his research has turned entirely to Mesozoic studies of the American Southwest, including work at the Ghost Ranch *Coelophysis* quarry in New Mexico, the Petrified Forest National Park in Arizona, and many sites elsewhere in New Mexico. In 1986 he organized the First International Symposium on Dinosaur Tracks and Traces in Albuquerque; with his wife Lynett, he has been coordinating the development of the Ruth Hall Museum of Paleontology at Ghost Ranch, Abiquin, New Mexico.

Mark Hallett (VOLUME I) is an artist, writer, and naturalist based in Pasadena, California. He teaches classes in zoological illustration at the Natural History Museum of Los Angeles County and biomedical illustration and anatomy at Otis Art Institute in Los Angeles. He has created numerous habitat murals for museums and zoos in California, including the San Diego Zoo, the San Diego Natural History Museum, and the Natural History Museum of Los Angeles County. He is illustrator and codesigner of *Zoobooks* (Wildlife Education, Ltd., San Diego), a series on living animals and extinct and endangered species; he created all the illustrations for the June 1985 issue on dinosaurs.

John R. Horner, Ph.D. (VOLUME II), who is Curator of Paleontology at the Museum of the Rockies, Montana State University, Bozeman, has led fossil collecting expeditions that have resulted in discoveries giving indication of communal nesting grounds and parental care of hatchlings in some species of dinosaurs. With James Gorman, he has written a popular book on *Maiasaura* or "good mother lizard," (*Maia: A Dinosaur Grows Up,* Museum of the Rockies, 1986) a species that he discovered and described. He was a 1986 recipient of the prestigious MacArthur Foundation Award and has also been awarded an honorary doctoral degree from the University of Montana.

Martin G. Lockley, Ph.D. (VOLUME I), Associate Professor of Geology at the University of Colorado in Denver, is conducting pioneering research on trackways of dinosaurs in the western United States. He is attempting to revive the lost art of animal tracking, to apply its techniques to the fossilized evidence of the movements of dinosaurs in all ancient habitats where they are preserved, and to devise methods of documenting the information contained in the tracks. He is finding that the tracks yield a census of life in dinosaur communities, including information about assemblages of dinosaurs, the behavior of individuals, and the ecosystems through which the animals moved.

Everett C. Olson, Ph.D., coeditor of this book, is Professor Emeritus of Zoology at the University of California at Los Angeles and member of the faculty of the Center for the Study of Evolution and The Origin of Life at UCLA. A specialist in vertebrate paleontology, he has authored numerous influential books and papers on the evolution of reptiles, vertebrate paleoecology, and the origins of mammals. He is a member of the National Academy of Sciences and Past President of the Society of Vertebrate Paleontology and the Society of Systematic Zoology. In 1980, the Paleontology Society honored Dr. Olson with their most prestigious award, the Paleontological Medal.

Kevin Padian, Ph.D. (VOLUME II), is Associate Professor of Paleontology and Biology at the University of California at Berkeley. His major interests include dinosaurs, pterosaurs, macroevolution, the systematics of reptiles, and the origins of major evolutionary features.

He was editor of *The Beginning of the Age of Dinosaurs* (Cambridge University Press, 1986). His current research projects include the taxonomic revision of the early pterosaurs and (with Paul E. Olsen) studies on the relationship between fossil footprints and the stance and gait of the trackmakers.

Gregory S. Paul (VOLUME II) is a Baltimore paleontologist and artist who has been studying and drawing dinosaurs since early childhood. He worked informally at Johns Hopkins University under Robert T. Bakker from 1977 to 1983, a period that he believes was critical to the development of his technical and aesthetic style. He was responsible for the paleontological design of AeroVironment's fully mobile half-sized model of *Quetzalcoatlus northropi*. Mr. Paul is author of a number of scientific papers on dinosaurs and has recently finished writing and illustrating a book on predatory dinosaurs of the world to be published by Simon and Schuster, New York.

J. Keith Rigby, Jr., Ph.D. (VOLUME II), is Assistant Professor in the Department of Earth Sciences, University of Notre Dame. He received his Ph.D. from Columbia University in 1977; his dissertation concerned Paleocene mammalian biostratigraphy. Since then he has conducted studies of continental stratigraphy and vertebrate paleontology throughout North America and Canada and has been involved in studies of European fossil vertebrates as well. In 1984 he found dinosaurs in deposits of Paleocene age; his paper in this book describes aspects of these and other more recent finds and their implications about the climate and habitat of the last of the dinosaurs.

Dale A. Russell, Ph.D. (VOLUME I), is Curator of Fossil Vertebrates at the National Museum of Natural Sciences, National Museums of Canada, in Ottawa. He received a doctoral degree in 1964 from Columbia University in New York, under the supervision of Edwin H. Colbert. His research interests include dinosaurian anatomy, faunistics and extinction, and the implications of the terrestrial fossil record for the evolution of extraterrestrial life. Dr. Russell is completing a book on the dinosaurs of North America to be published by the National Museum of Natural Sciences.

THE SCIENCE AND ART OF RESTORING THE LIFE APPEARANCE OF DINOSAURS AND THEIR RELATIVES
A Rigorous How-to Guide

GREGORY S. PAUL

*T*hat inherent uncertainties in the fossil record allow wide latitude in interpreting the life appearance of extinct animals is an unsubstantiated truism and one that hinders the practice and acceptance of paleontological restoration as a scientific discipline. It is also responsible for many inaccuracies that continue to plague dinosaur restorations.

Enough evidence is available to restore many dinosaur species with a very high degree of fidelity. This is especially true of certain duck-billed dinosaurs, whose abundant, articulated skeletons, trackways, and mummified remains allow them to be restored almost as precisely as some recently extinct animals. The skin of duckbills features dorsal midline frills and vertical shoulder folds. Among other dinosaurs, the horned dinosaurs bore unusually prominent scales and head-frill ornaments. Ankylosaurs show exceptional restorative potential because of their armor coverings. The body form of predatory dinosaurs is very like that of their avian descendants. All dinosaurs walked with a fully erect, narrow trackway gait. Most dinosaurs, even many giant forms, could run well; only sauropods, stegosaurs, and nodosaurs could not. Thecodonts, crocodilians, and pterosaurs offer important models for interpreting their dinosaur relatives, and vice versa.

Paleontological restoration is a discipline as valuable to the field as its other branches. At their best, when rendered with daring and boldness, restorations are also a form of art.

Detail of Figure 21

Figure 1. *Chasmosaurus "kaiseni"* skull studies showing the bare skull (top), restored muscles, keratin sheathes, and other soft tissues including pinnate cheeks, powerful frill-based jaw muscles, and hornlets and bosses (center), and restored life appearance (bottom) with skin extrapolated from skin preserved on other parts of body. Checklist 81.

The opening of the Como Bluff and Bernissart quarries in the 1870s provided artists with the first complete skeletons from which to restore dinosaurs. Since then artists have sometimes been ahead of the paleontologists. One fairly recent illustration showing a juvenile and adult *Triceratops* side by side was accompanied by a caption cautioning that such domestic scenes were as unlikely as they were appealing! Indeed, a frequent criticism of dinosaur restorations was that they made them too like birds or mammals. Although paleoillustrators have been vindicated on such points, restoring extinct animals remains an unappreciated side branch of paleontology. It is often assumed that because we cannot observe live dinosaurs we can at best restore them only approximately. This recalls the assertion of Comte (1835) that since astronomers could not directly sample stars they would never be able to know what they are made of. The result has been a damaging laissez-faire attitude about constructing dinosaurs, with skeletons still being mounted with wide-gauge trackways and dragging tails. Some paleontologists continue to approve restorations that cannot even contain the skeletons they are allegedly based upon; and museums are purchasing grossly inaccurate large-scale motion models. High-fidelity skeletal reconstructions of many basic dinosaurs, *Allosaurus*, *Brachiosaurus*, *Camarasaurus*, and *Stegosaurus* among them, have yet to be published.

In preparing a study on hadrosaur dinosaurs I was especially disturbed and chastened to find that no one, including myself, had correctly restored these most restorable of dinosaurs. Nearly complete, sometimes articulated skeletons and mummified remains allow some duck-billed species to be restored with a precision almost as high as those possible for some recently extinct animals whose life appearance is recorded by soft tissues and cave art.

THE BASICS

I am not attempting to present a definitive study on how to restore dinosaurs and their relatives but rather a brief overview to provide artists with basic information for accurately restoring archosaur anatomy and action. I have previously outlined the fundamentals of restoring prehistoric vertebrates (Paul 1984b; Paul and Chase, in press).

An original, detailed skeletal reconstruction based on the best available specimen or composite is very important for an accurate life restoration. Restorations based on previously published skeletal reconstructions or outline skeletal sketches usually prove to be seriously flawed. For this reason and because of past mistakes, I consider that most of my previously published works are no longer up to date, and the originals have been extensively revised. It is important to restore specific species and not only genera, even though there is often controversy about the identities of species and the specimens that represent them. It is always best to reconstruct the original or holotype specimen when possible. Also crucial are multiple-view reconstructions of at least one representative of each group. These reveal anatomical errors not always apparent in side view and detail the subject's three-dimensional structure. My skeletons are always posed in similar limb postures appropriate for their respective group, with the left hind limb pushing off. This facilitates both their preparation and comparison as does the drawing of each skeletal reconstruction to the same femur length (10.5 cm, except for pterosaurs). For these same reasons, humeri and femora are shown in direct lateral view instead of slightly everted as in life (compare Figs. 3c and 4f to 17).

McGowen (1979, 1982) properly cautions against drawing overly explicit conclusions about muscle form in extinct animals. However, much can still be done. Some of the more important muscles follow consistent origin-insertion patterns in most tetrapod groups, and some muscle scars can be positively identified. Muscle function also places limits on where muscles can be placed. In particular, muscles become ineffective when they are stretched much more than 1.3 times their resting length. Muscles should be profiled in black around the skeletal reconstructions as per Bakker (personal correspondence) and Scheele (1954). For studies of lizard, crocodile, bird, and mammal musculature see Fürbringer (1876), Romer (1923a, 1942, 1944), Knight (1947), L. S. Brown (1949), George and Berger (1966), and McGowen (1979, 1982).

Following the usual sources, I spent many years restoring dinosaurs as reptiles. But I sensed something was not right. Dinosaurs must have looked more like birds, rhinoceroses, and elephants than crocodiles and lizards. The growing evidence in the early 1970s that dinosaurs were more like birds and mammals was a revelation. But skin impressions show that over their avian-mammalian form was, at least in the big species, a reptilian veneer of scales, hornlets, and frills. Internally mammals are not the best models for detailed archosaur musculature because they evolved through an initial small-bodied "rough terrain and aboreal" phase. This has left their running descendants with unduly complex musculatures. Dinosaurs evolved in a much more straightforward manner from level-ground runners and retain simpler crocodile- and birdlike muscles. And dinosaurs had peculiarities of their own. Finally, to best know dinosaurs it is good to know their relatives, which are fascinating in their own right.

Heads Archosaur skulls are like those of reptiles and birds, and unlike those of mammals, in lacking facial muscles and having the skin directly appressed to the skull (Fig. 1). This feature makes them much easier to restore. Easily the most prominent skull muscle is the powerful posterior pterygoideus that wraps around and deepens the back third of the mandible. Jaw muscles bulge gently out of the skull openings behind the orbit and in thecodonts and saurischians also out of the preorbital opening and depression (Anderson 1936; Walker 1964; Norman 1985).

Dinosaur eyes were bird- or reptilelike not mammallike, so the iris is not surrounded by white. In big species the eyes were in the upper part of the orbit. Bony eye rings often show the actual size of the eye. Most dinosaurs had large eyes. Yet relative eye size decreases as animals get bigger, so I avoid the common tendency to make them overly large in big species. The eyes in juveniles and small species are proportionately much bigger, but even here restorations often exaggerate. Consider that the eye of the ostrich, the biggest among living terrestrial animals, does not appear oversize. The dinosaur's big eyes have been cited as evidence for both diurnal

(Russell 1973) and nocturnal habits (Russell and Seguin 1982). Actually big eyes are compatible with either life habit; it is the (in this case unknowable) structure of the retina that determines the type of light sensitivity.

The outer ear in dinosaurs is a depression between the quadrate and depressor mandibulae muscle.

Vertebral columns Almost all dinosaur necks naturally articulate in a birdlike S curve. Thecodont and crocodilian necks are only very gently curved, and those of pterosaurs seem intermediate. Because the occipital condyle points somewhat downward the head is held at a sharp angle to the neck in birds, most dinosaurs, and pterosaurs. In thecodonts, crocodilians, diplodocids, and ceratopsians the occipital condyle and head are in a straighter line with the neck. Large zygapophyses that remain articulated over a wide range of motion indicate that archosaur necks were generally quite flexible. Powerful side neck muscles often formed a contour over the weaker ventral muscles. Since no bony elements are directly involved, the muscles under the midneck are among the most difficult to estimate. I arbitrarily make them shallow.

In many reptiles, mammals, and birds the trunk vertebrae articulate in a straight line. Thecodonts, crocodilians, pterosaurs, and dinosaurs differ in having more strongly beveled dorsals that form a dorsally convex arch. Small zygapophyses and in many cases ossified interspinal ligaments indicate that dinosaurs had stiff backs. The sacrals generally continue the line of the dorsal column.

It cannot be overemphasized that of the many thousands of dinosaur trackways, quadrupedal and bipedal, only a tiny minority show tail-drag marks (Fig. 2b–f; Lockley, this book). All dinosaurs carried their tails clear of the ground, even the whip-tailed sauropods and club-tailed ankylosaurs. Trackways indicate that many thecodonts also carried their tails clear of the ground (Fig. 2a). Pretensed upper tail ligaments probably held the tail up at little energy cost. Dinosaur tail muscles and fat may not have bulged beyond the limits of the bones so they would not overload the tail, and this is confirmed by hadrosaur tail-skin impressions

Figure 2. Top: Trackways of derived thecodont (a), large theropod (b), prosauropod (c), sauropod (d), nodosaur (e), and iguanodont (f), drawn to same stride length. Note that there are no tail drag marks and that the hands are always hollow at the base and facing partly outwards. Bottom: Restored hands of sauropod *Brachiosaurus brancai* (g), nodosaur *Sauropelta edwardsi* (h), and hadrosaur (i), not to same scale. Data from Janensch (1961), Haubold (1971), Baird (1980), Currie (1983), Carpenter (1984), and Bird (1985).

(B. Brown 1916; Horner 1984). Large zygapophyses indicate that most thecodonts and dinosaurs had fairly flexible, but not serpentine, tails.

Ribcages, bellies, and hips Like those of crocodilians and birds, the anterior ribs of dinosaurs are usually strongly swept back in articulated dinosaur skeletons of all types (Osborn 1912; B. Brown 1916, Maryanska 1977; Norman 1985: 43, 61, 90, 103, 121, 144), in thecodonts (Ewer 1965: fig. 20; Cruickshank 1972; Romer 1972), and in pterosaurs (Eaton 1910: pl. VII; Wellnhofer 1970, 1975). This is little noticed, and many dinosaur skeletons are mounted with vertical anterior ribs. Normally the chest is slab sided, and since the rib heads are offset swinging them forward overbroadens the chest and misarticulates the shoulder girdle. The belly ribs tend to be more vertical, but this con-

dition is variable. Dinosaur trunk vertebrae and ribs form a short, fairly rigid box, with the shoulder and hip girdles close together so that the trunk musculature is rather light, like that of a bird. The longer, more flexible trunks of thecodonts indicate more powerful muscles. In all archosaurs the iliocostalis muscles continue the profile of the iliac blade onto the trunk.

All herbivores must have large digestive tracts to constantly contain the large bulk of plant material needed to sustain the healthy gut flora critical to plant digestion. Spacious posterior ribcages and hadrosaur mummies (B. Brown 1916) confirm that herbivorous dinosaurs have big bellies, so restorations that show them with hollow bellies are incorrect. In sharp contrast are big predators that gorged at a carcass, then fasted until hungry enough to hunt again. The poorly ossified, jointed abdominal ribs of predatory thecodonts and theropods are flexible, and these animals should be given hollow bellies when shown hunting.

The digestive tract and reproductive organs exit behind the ischium not under the pubis as indicated by M. Hallett (in Wexo 1985).

The dinosaur hip, especially the theropod's with its long downwardly projecting pubis and ischium, has long perplexed artists (Figs. 11, 14). Since the pubes and ischia of theropods are narrow and united along most or all of their midline, they bar the guts from between these two bones. Therefore, they were connected only by a thin tension sheet of connective tissue. To have been most effective this sheet should have stretched in a gentle concave arc between the tips of the two elements. As in living reptiles the lower tail muscles should also have run in a gentle tension curve from the tip of the ischium to the chevrons, and this is confirmed by hadrosaur mummies (B. Brown 1916; Currie personal communication). The side of the pubis had only a thin muscle running up to the upper end of the femur, and the side of the ischial rod was unmuscled. The hips of some thecodonts with long pubes are similar (Fig. 8b), and prosauropod and sauropod hips are built on the same basic plan except that they are broader (Figs. 15, 17). So the derived-thecodont saurischian lower hip was a laterally flattened tension brace unconnected to the thighs. In protobirds and ornithischians the pubis was swung backward parallel to the ischium, slinging the guts between the legs (Figs. 13, 18–20, 23, 25). In these the lower hip was a posteriorly tapering belly between the thighs. The dinosaur pubis and ischium were not submerged in flesh as often shown, but the ischium or its tip should not project out as in some restorations. Such restorations may have been inspired by the externally prominent ischia of kangaroos, but their ancestors had the usual reduced mammalian tail and are not good models for dinosaurs.

Shoulder girdles and fore limbs Dinosaur coracoids articulated with the grooved edges of a cartilagenous anterior sternum, which is in front of the paired posterior sternals (Norman 1980). The latter articulated with the first long pair of dorsal ribs via a short sternal rib. This allows the position of the shoulder girdle to be determined with confidence. Because the anterior ribs were backswept, the coracoid was under the neck-trunk juncture, not in front of it. Most distressing are reconstructions showing the coracoid jammed against the ribcage (Santa-Luca et al. 1976). In the narrow-chested thecodonts and most dinosaurs the plane of the scapulacoracoid was fairly parasagittal as in chameleons. The exceptions are protobirds and pterosaurs whose very birdlike retroverted coracoids faced anteriorly. In side view thecodont and dinosaur scapulacoracoids were usually fairly vertical, as in most tetrapods, and not horizontal. Because of their elongated, retroverted coracoids, only pterosaurs, protobirds, and birds have horizontal scapula blades.

Articulated skeletons show that scapulacoracoid orientation is variable in quadrupedal dinosaurs. This is compatible with the chameleonlike scapulacoracoid rotation suggested by Bakker (1975, this book). Dinosaurs lack a clavicle-interclavicle brace. This can be explained only as a means of freeing the coracoid to glide fore and aft in the sternal groove. Likewise chameleons, turtles, crocodilians, and mammals have freed the shoulder girdle by unbracing it (Peterson 1984; Nicholls and Russell 1985). Nicholls and Russell, however, are incorrect in attributing scapular mobility to all birdlike theropods; in many the large fused furculae and big sternal plates immobilized the shoulder girdle (Fig. 14; Barsbold 1983; Paul and Carpenter, in preparation). Note that the vertically oriented scapulacoracoid does not cut off the throat or perform other anatomical violations as it swings forward, contrary to Bennett and Dalzell (1973). Scapular rotation is important because the shoulder joints swing fore and aft relative to one another during the limb cycle, a mammallike attribute.

Contention still surrounds the issue of dinosaur fore-limb posture. This is unfortunate since trackways of all species show the narrow fore-print gauge typical of a fully erect gait (Fig. 2c–f; Bakker 1971a; Lockley, this book). Crucial to the issue is the relative orientation of the shoulder joint. Especially informative in this regard are chameleon shoulder girdles, which are so amazingly like those of dinosaurs that one found in Mesozoic sediments would be identified as a tiny dinosaur (Fig. 3b). The chameleon shoulder glenoid is much more inwardly directed than in crocodilians and lizards, partly because the scapulacoracoid is flatter relative to the body wall. As a consequence chameleons have a much more vertical humerus action (Peterson 1984; Bannister 1984). With the scapulacoracoid also in a nearly parasagittal plane the scapular portion of the dinosaur shoulder glenoid actually faces slightly inward (Fig. 3c–d). This can only mean a nearly vertical humerus action, with the elbow tucked in close to the body. This is confirmed by the orientation of dinosaur hand prints, which, as Carpenter (1982) explains, invariably face outward (see Fig. 2c–f). Facing both the hand and elbow outward requires that the radius and ulna be uncrossed, but this is not possible in dinosaurs because they have moderately crossed, partly or completely interlocking radii and ulnae (Fig. 3c–d, note that the radius articulates with the outer humerus condyle and the inner wrist bones; a number of recent skeletal mounts do not reflect this basic fact). In fact a sprawling gait requires freely rotating lower arm elements that will not twist the foot on the ground as the arm pivots backward. Detailed articulations show that dinosaur elbows are only moderately bowed out some fifteen or more degrees, excepting rectigrades in which it is less (large deltoid crests obscure this elbow eversion in the skeletal front views, and these show the minimum elbow eversions of high speeds). The beveled end of the radius bows the wrist inward a little. Ungulates have similar limbs (see front views in Nowak and Paradiso 1983; Norman 1985: 139).

Trackways prove that the advanced rauisuchid thecodonts also had narrow trackways and outwardly facing hands (Fig. 2a). With more outwardly facing shoulder joints and flexible radii and ulnae their elbow was more bowed out (Fig. 8). More primitive thecodonts, such as *Euparkeria*, and eurythrosuchids and phytosaurs had wider, semierect fore limbs; the ancestral chasmosaurs were full sprawlers (Bakker 1971a; see Lockley, this book, on phytosaur fore-limb tracks). Comparative manipulation of bird and pterosaur fore limbs shows that the latter could be used for ground locomotion (contra Padian 1983). The out- and upward facing shoulder joint means a sprawling fore limb, with the elbow flexed down ninety degrees from the horizontal humerus to give the hands a narrow trackway. That even the marine *Pteranodon* retains fully functional fingers confirms that it moved with its hands.

Having dealt with transverse fore-limb posture, we turn to fore and aft posture. Most dinosaurs are "primitive" in having backwardly directed shoulder glenoids and humerus heads that wrap far onto the back of the humerus (Bakker 1974). This flexes the shoulder and elbow, so that the humerus slopes down and backward as in ungulates (Fig. 3c). Because of the shoulder girdle's mobility and the open shoulder joint the humerus could protract to vertical (contra Bennett and Dalzell 1973).

In nodosaurs, sauropods, and stegosaurs the shoulder glenoid faces much more downward, and the humerus head does not wrap as far backward. Also, the distal humeral condyles do not wrap as far forward as in other dinosaurs. These are derived characters, and they show that the humerus was vertical and the elbow was straight in these elephant-limbed or rectigrade dinosaurs (Fig. 3d; Bakker 1971a).

All dinosaur and pterosaur hands were either digitigrade or unguligrade, and the wrist was stiffly held straight or close to it during the propulsive stroke. None had the flat, plantigrade hands retained in thecodonts and crocodilians. All archosaurs could hyperflex the wrist; even elephants flick the wrist back ninety degrees to clear the hand during recovery. It is important to remember that no archosaur had hands that looked like the feet. Due partly to different bone structures their fore feet always lack a heavy central pad and are hollow behind, giving them a distinctive half-moon shape (Fig. 2c–i). In hadrosaurs, iguanodonts, sauropods, and stegosaurs the fingers are united into a pseudohoof in that they are encased in a single lunate pad, with most or all of the single hooves lost. A very distinctive character of theropods, prosauropods, and some sauropods and ornithischians (including iguanodonts) is the big clawed, inwardly-divergent-when-extended thumb weapon. It was

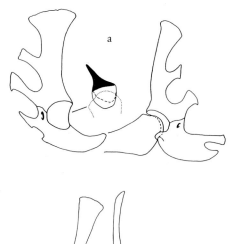

often held clear of the ground when walking. Birds retain this medially divergent thumb as the feathered alula, or wing slot. Thecodonts, crocodilians, and pterosaurs lack inwardly pointing thumbs.

The scapula's upper end was capped with a short cartilage extension and formed a gentle contour. In most dinosaurs the scapular acromion process probably supported a scapular-sternal ligament, which in turn supported the clavicular deltoids. The proximal end of the humerus bulged out a little, and in many but not all dinosaurs a very large deltoid crest formed a prominent contour along the entire length. The triceps was a prominent contour muscle. The scar for the latissimus dorsi is unusually far down, opposite the deltoid crest's lower end where it formed a prominent contour above the arm pit. Hand flexors and extensors bunched around the elbow and operated the hand via tendons; the wrist formed a bulge.

Hind limbs Hip morphology suggests that chasmosaur hind limbs were sprawling, and that euparkerids, eurythrosuchids, and phytosaurs were semierect (Fig. 8a; Bakker 1971a). But trackways indicate that phytosaurs had more erect legs than thought (Lockley, this book). In aetosaurs, postosuchids, and rauisuchids the upper ilium and hip socket are swung out over the femoral head so that the femur could work in a nearly vertical plane (Fig. 8b; Bonaparte 1981, 1983; downwardly flaring sacral ribs show that postosuchids have this hip design, contra Chatterjee 1985). Narrow-gauge trackways confirm their erect gait. The protodinosaur ornithosuchids, protocrocodilians, and early pterosaurs have rather dinosaurlike hip joints that indicate a fairly erect hind limb. Advanced pterosaurs, however, have secondarily reverted to semierect legs.

The crocodilianlike thecodont knee appears to be flexed, but as in crocodilians the hind limbs are so flexible that the femur can retract well past vertical and the knee can straighten.

Heerden (1979) and Martin (1984) suggest that prosauropods and protobirds walked with a wide, semierect gait. But, like those of all dinosaurs, trackways show that prosauropod hind limbs followed a narrow-gauge trackway (Baird 1980; Olsen and Galton 1984). The characters

Figure 3. A comparison of left shoulder joint orientation, fore-limb posture, and joint articulation in the lizards *Iguana* (a) and *Chamaeleo* (b), the flexed-limbed dinosaur *Triceratops horridus*, USNM 4842 and AMNH 970 (c), and the rectigrade *Brachiosaurus brancai*, HMN SII and HMN Sa9 (d, compare to Fig. 17). Stippling indicates the ulnar articular facets for the humeral condyles as distinct from the olecranon process. Not to scale.

Heerden cited as evidence of a semierect gait are actually the same as those found in the fully erect birds, *Archaeopteryx,* and most other dinosaurs. These all share similar limbs in which the knee is bowed out moderately, especially as it swings forward and clears the gut (the skeletal back views show the minimal, high-speed knee eversion), and the ankle is bowed inward slightly (see the ostrich in Muybridge [1887] 1957; pigeon in Cracraft 1971; Santa-Luca 1980). Ungulates are also similar (see rear views in Muybridge [1887] 1957). In the rectigrade sauropods and stegosaurs the knee was less bowed out. Knight (in Massey-Czerkas and Glut 1982: 35, 80), Parker (in Swinton 1970), and Spinar and Burian (1972) occasionally splayed out dinosaur hind limbs too much.

In side view, inadequately considered hind-limb action afflicts many restorations. Newman (1970), Galton (1970), Hotton (1980), Cooper (1980), and Hallett (in Wexo 1985) give varying accounts of how bone strengthening around the hip socket affects posture and limb action. The greatest normal stress in animals is up- and forward as the hind limb pushes the body in the same direction. Severe abnormal stresses include a back- and upward shock if a foot missteps. Hence, dinosaur hip joints are well strengthened both fore (sometimes by sacral ribs, Maryanska and Osmolska 1984), and aft, as well as above. Hip-joint stressing tells us therefore little about posture.

What tells us more is the expanded posterior portion of the acetabulum, or antitrochanter. Also found in birds, it remains fully articulated with the femoral head as the femur swings from about sixty degrees forward of vertical to about vertical (except for sauropods and stegosaurs). Contrary to usual opinion, photographs and films show that femoral action is this extensive in fast-running birds (see Fig. 5; Ricciuti 1979; Boswell and Mansfield 1981; Chadwick 1983). Either rearing the body up too high or hyperretracting the femur partly disarticulates the hip joint. It also overshortens the ischial-based femoral retractors. Rearing, therefore, is tolerable only at slow speeds.

Charig (1972) argues that normally walking saurischian-hipped dinosaurs tilted up to avoid a supposed "knee-knocking-on-the-pubis" problem.

However, much of the pubioischiofemoralis internus functions to keep the femur erect in these dinosaurs rather than to protract it, and plenty of other muscles are available to protract the femur forward of the pubis.

Dinosaur and pterosaur knees are very birdlike. A large "roller" inner femoral condyle bears most of the load. Meanwhile a thin angular outer condyle runs in a groove between the tibia and fibula and prevents the knee from twisting about its long axis (Fig. 4a–c). In most post-thecodont archosaurs the knee cannot be straightened because to do so would rotate the outer condyle out of its groove and leave the knee open to complete dislocation. This is true even of such giants as *Tyrannosaurus rex, Triceratops,* and *Shantungosaurus.* The orientation of the hip and knee joints shows that most dinosaurs had bird- or ungulatelike femoral posture and action in which the knee always stayed flexed (Fig. 4a–c, e) and the femur never retracted past vertical (Tarsitano's 1983 restoration of dinosaur hind-limb action is especially out of line with this evidence). Indeed overall limb action must have been very like that of fast birds and mammals with the femur providing the main propulsive stroke (Fig. 5).

In sauropods and stegosaurs the antitrochanter is reduced or absent, and so the femur can retract past vertical. In addition, the fibula-calcaneum unit is longer than the tibia-astragalus so that the fibula head can rise above the tibia head (Fig. 4d) and brace the outer femoral condyle even when the knee is straight. The femur is therefore vertical in these rectigrades (Fig. 4f).

Most dinosaurs and pterosaurs had simple, birdlike hinge-jointed ankles that hyperflexed to clear the foot from the ground during recovery. The sauropod's and stegosaur's very short, broad metatarsi and toes, backed by a very large pad, indicate, however, a fixed ankle. Dinosaur metatarsi were always tightly interbound; the frequency with which articulated pterosaur metatarsals are splayed apart suggests increased suppleness. Like the hand, all dinosaur and pterosaur feet are digitigrade or unguligrade, never plantigrade; nor were they ever semiunguligrade like ostriches—certain trackways that suggest so are reflecting the distri-

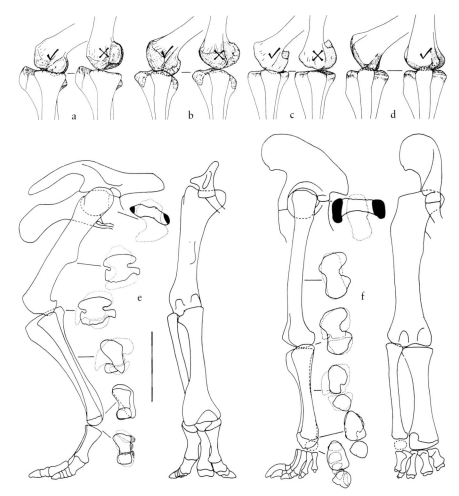

Figure 4. Top: The articulation of the left knee in the giant flexed-jointed *Tyrannosaurus rex*, CM 9380 (a), *Triceratops horridus*, USNM 4842 (b), and *Shantungosaurus giganteus*, PMNH 5 (c), and in the rectigrade *Stegosaurus ungulatus* YPM 1858 (d). On the left the knees are flexed with the outer femoral condyle running in the groove made by the fibula and tibia. On the right the knee is straightened, which works only in *Stegosaurus* in which the fibula is proximally extended and continues to brace the outer femoral condyle. Bottom: A comparison of hind-limb posture and joint articulation in the flexed-limbed dinosaur *Kritosaurus incurvimanus*, ROM 764 (e) and the rectigrade *Brachiosaurus brancai*, HMN specimens (f, compare to Fig. 17). Stippling indicates hypotarsi; data in part from Janensch (1961), Ostrom and McIntosh (1966, especially pl. 49) and Hu (1973). Not to scale.

bution of pressure along the toes (Thulborn and Wade 1984). Most dinosaurs probably let their toes droop during recovery as do the big ground birds (toe clenching is limited to perching birds). Sauropod and stegosaur toes were relatively immobile. The four-toed basal predatory dinosaurs, prosauropods, segnosaurs, and some ornithopods bear large hind claws. They and the big-clawed early theropods may have balanced on their robust tails and kicked out like dinosaurian kangaroos (Marx 1978: fig. 1; Bakker personal communication). Thecodont metatarsi and feet were always supple and plantigrade, and the complex ankles are rather mammallike with a long calcaneal tuber in the heel. Suggestions by Walker (1964), Sill (1974), and Chatterjee (1985) that advanced thecodonts were digitigrade are not supported by the typically thecodontian ankles and feet found in these animals. In dinosaurs toe 5 is reduced to a splint or lost.

The tail-based caudofemoralis femoral retractor muscle forms a prominent contour (its profile is seen under the more superficial muscles in muscle restorations), excepting, of course, in the tailless pterydactyloids and birds. The evolution of the archosaur ischium and the femoral retractors it supports is very interesting. In basal thecodonts and pterosaurs the ischium is a short, broad lizardlike apron that anchored a number of femoral retractors. The ischial rod found in advanced thecodonts and most dinosaurs is too slender to have anchored femoral retractors; in addition, such distally placed muscles would have been badly overstretched during normal limb action. Instead, the rod is a tension brace. In protobirds and birds, who have returned to the thecodont condition, the rod is lost as the tail is reduced.

Lizards and crocodilians are good models for restoring thecodont hind limb and foot muscles,

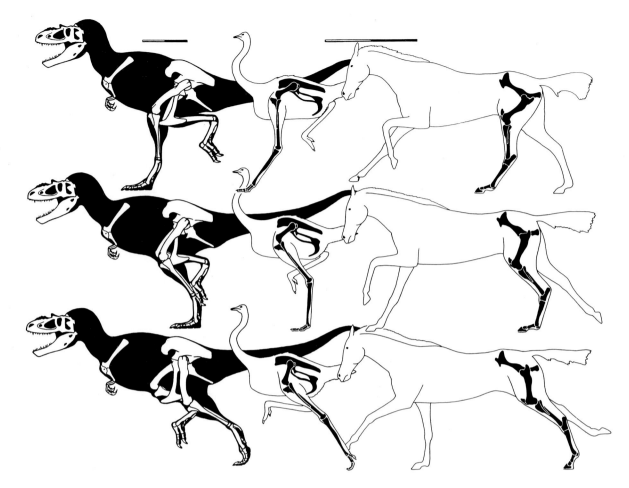

Figure 5. Comparison of hind-limb action in fast-running thoroughbred, ostrich, and *Albertosaurus libratus*. Bone positions are approximate; note the similarity of the animals' hind-limb action including extensive femoral action. Scale bars equal 1 meter. Data for ostrich from Chadwick (1983) and Boswell and Mansfield (1981); data for horse from pl. 71 in Muybridge ([1887] 1957).

and the achilles tendon is very prominent above the calcaneum tuber. Pterosaurs and dinosaurs differ greatly in having much more bird- or ungulatelike hind-limb muscles. In particular, the thigh is laterally flattened but antero-posteriorly broad, a fact recognized by Romer (1923b, 1927). One of Knight's greatest and most persistent errors was to show dinosaurs with narrow, reptilelike thighs (in Massey-Czerkas and Glut 1982). The anterior expansion of the iliac blade supported an enlarged, birdlike anterior iliotibialis in sauropods, segnosaurs, and theropods, and not just ornithischians. In pterosaurs and most dinosaurs the knee's large cnemial crest and the birdlike feet show that a powerful "drumstick" of extensor and flexor muscles operated the feet via long tendons (Bakker in Russell 1973; Glut 1982; Padian 1983). The gastrocnemius and achilles tendon were prominent as they ran behind the leg and ankle to the foot. As in birds the ankle joint must have been very prominent,

with grooves running between the upper and lower tarsals.

Exceptions to the normal pattern are again the sauropods and stegosaurs. There is a tendency to restore their limbs as heavily muscled pillars, but since the foot is immobile the shank muscles that operate it are weak. Indeed the shin was hardly muscled at all, as in humans and elephants (see Knight 1947). The ankle joint was buried in the great foot pad.

Speed A pack of running tyrannosaurs attacking a herd of charging ceratopsians makes for a dynamic restoration (Fig. 6). The image, however, is difficult to accept because we are accustomed to a modern world that is biased against big runners; there are no giant predators, so there is little incentive for big animals to be fast. Indeed, it is widely, but not universally, accepted that stress loads and design constraints prevent very large animals from running.

Actually the ability to run is normal among terrestrial animals. A run is when all the limbs leave the ground simultaneously in a ballistic suspended phase, including hopping, the bipedal run, the trot, pace, and various gallops. Among living medium-sized and big animals only elephants and tortoises cannot run. In fact, most animals run very well, better than we humans. As for size, no stress, scaling, or morphological analysis establishing that big size does bar high speeds has been published. Scaling, mechanical, and energetic studies do indicate that big animals enjoy important advantages over small animals and can be fast (Heglund et al. 1982; McMahon 1984; Lindstedt et al. 1985). Indeed, a 3.5-metric-ton white rhino can gallop (Guggisberg 1966), and 1.8-metric-ton black rhinos are reported to outsprint horses (Muybridge [1887] 1957). The real question is not whether dinosaurs could run, but whether any could not.

Elephants and tortoises cannot run because they have very strange limbs, with fixed ankles that cannot rotate more than a few degrees. The effects of this can be simulated by trying to run on your heels alone. Medium-sized and larger animals with flexible ankles that can push the body into a long, suspended phase can run; there are no exceptions.

Among dinosaurs only sauropods and stegosaurs have a fixed ankle; the limbs of other dinosaurs are of the peculiar columnar elephantine type (rectigrade) compatible with a slow, ambling gait (Fig. 7; Muybridge [1887] 1957; Bakker 1971a, b, c). Coombs (1975) suggested that sauropods were slower than elephants because they lack elbow and ankle leverage, criticism sometimes leveled at dinosaurs in general. It is contradicted by the fact that quadrupedal dinosaurs have large olecranon processes and hypotarsi.

All other dinosaurs have fairly long birdlike ankles and feet and so could run. Many trackways show small to very large dinosaurs running (Farlow 1981; Lockley et al. 1983; Thulborn and Wade 1984; Matsukawa and Obata 1985). As with humans, however, a flexible ankle does not guarantee high speeds of more than fifty kilometers per hour.

A basic fast running limb design includes long bird- or ungulatelike limbs with powerful, proximally concentrated muscles, deep shoulder and hip sockets, cylindrical flexed spring-action joints, tibiae and metatarsi that together make up at least ninety percent of the femur's length, large olecranons and hypotarsi, and laterally compressed, functionally three-toed, lightly padded, digitigrade or unguligrade feet. All living animals with such limbs run well. Excepting sauropods, stegosaurs, and to a certain degree nodosaurs, all dinosaurs—including the biggest ornithopods, ceratopsids, and tyrannosaurs—also have all of these limb adaptations (Bakker 1971a, Paul, in press, a). Tyrannosaurs are especially important because they share the same limb anatomy as the ostrich-mimic theropods (McMahon 1984: figs. 4–9). Far from being dinosaurian tortoises and elephants, most dinosaurs were involved in a predator-prey size and speed race. It is not surprising therefore that one trackway appears to show a small bipedal dinosaur running some seventy kilometers per hour (suggestions by Welles [1971] and Thulborn and Wade [1984] that a hyperlong limbed walking dinosaur made this track are unsupported by any evidence). Especially unacceptable are suggestions that even small, gracile dinosaurs were built only for walking and speeds of thirteen kilometers per hour (Halstead and Halstead 1981; Hotton 1980).

Integument and claws Skin impressions are known from a number of large dinosaurs. They show that dinosaur scales were always nonbony, mosaic patterned, and never overlapping. Even in big species the skin appears to have been thin. One hadrosaur mummy indicates that the thigh skin made a smooth unfolded transition onto the trunk, and this may have been true of other dinosaurs as well. Prominent frills and skin folds are sometimes preserved; these, dewlaps, wattles, and other soft display organs may have been more common than we realize.

Some suggest that since big dinosaurs are known to have naked skin, small dinosaurs and thecodonts should have the same. Especially fascinating in this regard are the preserved insulation coats of some small archosaurs. These include the long body contour scales in longisquamid thecodonts (Sharov 1970; not to be confused with the elongated "dorsal scales"), pterosaur fur (Sharov

1971), and *Archaeopteryx*'s famous feathers. I do not know of a single case of mosaic scales in small dinosaurs or thecodonts. (It is enlightening to consider that if future nonhumanoid paleontologists living in a nonmammalian world find only human, rhino and elephant skin impressions, they might conclude that all mammals were naked skinned!) There is skin preserved in small *Thescelosaurus*, but Gilmore (1915) noted that it had a "punctured" instead of a scaled surface (this impression is not currently accessible). The difference of this small ornithopod's skin from the big ornithopod's indicates that it served a different purpose. The punctured surface may have supported an insula-tive covering. If small archosaurs were so insulated, their avian relationships strongly suggest that they were feathered. Thulborn (1985) speculates that dinosaur feathers may have been contoured rather than degenerate and furlike as suggested by Feduccia (1980). Either is possible. It is also possible that the juveniles of large species were insulated, perhaps in down, which they shed as they matured.

Articulated armor tells us much about the outer appearance of some thecodonts, crocodilians, and dinosaurs. Armor plates, hornlets, bosses, and skull rugosities are almost always enlarged by horn (keratin). The bony cores of claws and hooves are likewise enlarged by horn coverings, and these are often but not always worn down at the edges or tip.

Color This aspect of restoration is most asked about, least knowable, and least important. I often do not decide the dinosaur's color until I have completed the background and see what looks best. A light tone might appear advantageous for large animals in hot habitats, but tropical naked-skinned animals such as elephants, rhinos, humans, monitors, and crocodilians are dark, as an ultraviolet radiation screen. Russell (1977) suggests that color-sighted dinosaurs should have borne color camouflage patterns. This may be correct, but earth-tinged mammals blend well into backgrounds before color-sensitive human eyes. Also significant is that big reptiles and birds tend to be earth tinged despite their color vision. The big archosaur's scales (as opposed to the bare skin of big mammals) could carry bold patterns, like those of giraffes and zebras. Small archosaurs are the best candidates for bright motifs. Archosaurs of all sizes may have used specific color displays for intraspecific communication or for startling predators. Crests, frills, skin folds, and taller neural spines would be natural bases for vivid, even iridescent, display colors, especially in the breeding season. But remember, except for the improbability of gaudy colors on the big species, any color pattern is both speculative and possible.

THE ARCHOSAUR GROUPS

Thecodonts Most thecodonts are rather long, low, crocodile-shaped animals, except that their skulls

Figure 6. "An *Albertosaurus libratus* Pair Invites a *Monoclonius* (= *Styracosaurus*) *albertensis* Herd to Dinner, The Latter Firmly Decline." Like most big dinosaurs, the bird-limbed tyrannosaurs and rhino-like ceratopsids were built for speed; their combat is unrivaled in the modern world. The locale is a cattail marsh in the Judith River Formation. Checklist 68.

are deep and narrow, like those of dinosaurs (Fig. 8). Their trackways, big heads and necks, and fairly strong fore limbs show that they were usually quadrupedal, except for the short fore-limbed *Postosuchus* (Chatterjee 1985). Long, well-muscled, vertically flexible (not laterally as in lizards) dorsal columns suggest that their fastest gait was a bounding, crocodilelike gallop, even in the giant forms (Fig. 8b; Zug 1974). The supple-limbed, flat-footed, galloping, predatory thecodonts were archosaurian "bear/crocs," quite different from the birdlike predatory dinosaurs.

Many thecodonts are restored with transversely rounded skull roofs, whereas articulated skulls are usually flat as in other archosaurs. At least some thecodonts such as *Saurosuchus* (Fig. 8b) had horn decorations on their skull. Phytosaurs have highly sculpted skulls very like the crocodilians they so closely mimic.

The hands and feet have five free digits, except for a few species that lack the outer toe. The outer finger and toe were usually divergent grasping digits, as in many lizards. Claws are usually rather small, the hind feet pointed straight ahead or outward.

Most thecodonts have a row of paired scutes running along their backbone and sometimes underneath their tails. The well-known aetosaurs differ from most thecodonts in being big-bellied, small-skulled, heavily armored herbivores. Phytosaurs too bear a heavy, in their case crocodilelike, armor and are also known from many excellent skeletons. They and aetosaurs are among the most restorable of archosaurs.

The reconstruction of the *Gracilosuchus stipanicicorum* skull by Brinkman (1981) is at odds with the complete and little-crushed skull of the Museum of Comparative Zoology (MCZ 4117) with its aetosaurlike posterior skull (Romer 1972; Lewis personal communication). The skeletal reconstruction of Chatterjee (1985) of *Postosuchus kirkpatricki* is too short in the vertebral column by fifty percent. Note that ornithosuchids, which were protodinosaurs, were always small, never big as suggested by Walker (1964).

Pterosaurs I agree with Padian (1983) that pterosaur wing membranes did not connect with the hind limbs and that the hind limbs folded together for streamlining in normal flight (Fig. 9). There is evidence that the tailless pterodactyloids had an auxiliary membrane behind the hind limb (Broili 1938; Wellnhofer 1970; Paul in Parrish 1986: 79). Pterodactyloids have supple humanlike ball-and-socket hip joints and may have used the hind-limb membrane for special maneuvers, especially landings. Impressions also indicate the presence of webbed hind feet (Broili 1938; Wellnhofer 1970, 1975). These may have been used as air brakes. Instead of projecting out, the free fingers were probably appressed to the wing finger during flight for streamlining. Padian (1983) shows that most pterosaurs were powered flappers. Indeed, even the giant pterosaurs retain the smaller pterosaur's flapping adaptations, including large deltoid crests. The enormous deltoid crest, elbow joint, and carpal block of *Quetzalcoatlus* are especially contrary to

Figure 7. "*Brachiosaurus brancai* Herd." Unlike most dinosaurs, elephantine sauropods such as this were not built for speed—they would rather fight than flee. The locale is the Tendaguru Formation; araucarian and other conifers make up the flora. This drawing, which has been extensively revised (for earlier versions see Gould [1978, 1980] and Battaglia [1979]), is my favorite dinosaur restoration. Checklist 77.

the streamlining expected in soarers and suggest that even the biggest pterosaurs were predominantly flappers.

Unlike broad-winged, slow-flying bats, in which the fore limb does not blend into the wing membrane, the narrow-winged, fast-flying molossid bats use fur and muscles to streamline the wing bones into the membrane (Vaughan and Bateman 1980). The narrow-winged pterosaurs were fast flyers and probably did the same (Fig. 9). Connective tissue probably continued the fore wing a short distance outside of the wrist. AeroVironment's work on *Quetzalcoatlus* aerodynamics (Mac-Cready 1985; Parrish 1986) suggests that pterosaurs had wings like frigate birds or gulls, with a sharp reflex at the base of the wing finger and a membrane that was broadest behind this reflex. This makes them exceptionally graceful creatures.

Most pterosaurs, even those with teeth, had horn beaks lengthening their jaws. Pterosaur necks have too few vertebrae for the skull to be pulled back over the trunk as in some birds. The sharp angle between the head and neck suggests a gently upcurved neck.

Padian (1983) argues that all pterosaur hips were united along the ventral midline. Many were, but three-dimensionally preserved specimens show that *Rhamphorhynchus* has splayed out, birdlike lower hip elements (specimens in the Mineralogisk Museum, Copenhagen [MMK 1891.738 in Wellnhofer 1975] and Raymond Alf Museum, Los Angeles). Padian (1983) shows that pterosaur hind limbs are powerful running organs. On the other hand, big-headed yet tailless pterodactyloids are not well adapted for bipedality because they lack the anterior migration of the hip joint and the posterior migration of the belly that helps birds balance over their hind limbs. Their fastest gait was probably a fast quadrupedal trot. The long-tailed rhamphorhynchoids may have been more bipedal, especially *Dimorphodon* in which the elbow to finger base distance is too short for the fore limb to have been used on the ground.

The three short fingers bear large recurved claws. The four normal toes have small claws, in rhamphorhynchoids the very long, unclawed fifth toe may have helped support a web.

The aquatic sediments in which pterosaurs are found, the paucity of terrestrial remains, their often peculiar feeding adaptations, and their apparently webbed feet suggest that they were generally either shorebirds or oceanic. There is little evidence that they experienced a terrestrial radiation like passerine birds. Even *Quetzalcoatlus*, found only in terrestrial deposits, probably patrolled water courses, like a three-meter-tall stork, picking up fish and small animals. Its slender, two-meter

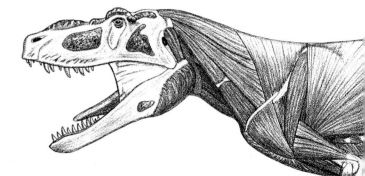

beak, with only thin bars around the external nares, is too weak for regular scavenging (Parrish 1986). Artists persist in showing *Pteranodon* flying above the head of *Tyrannosaurus rex* and *Triceratops*. Yet not only is *Pteranodon* pre-Maastrichtian, it is like the albatross in being known only from marine deposits.

The beaked, water-loving pterosaurs were probably birdlike, specifically shorebirdlike, in appearance. Yet there is still something of the bat in these quadrupedal, wing-membraned beings. The upper surface of the wing membrane must have been dark for protection against ultraviolet radiation (restricted blood flow in the membrane and aircooling would prevent overheating), the undersides were probably a pale sky-color for camouflage.

A realistic, half-sized model of *Quetzalcoatlus northropi* that W. Langston and I provided the paleodesign for has achieved flapping flight and is the first fully mobile reproduction of an extinct tetrapod (MacCready 1985; Parrish 1986). Cross-scaling of various sized *Quetzalcoatlus* specimens shows that the wings were eleven meters across (Langston personal communication). The biggest

Pteranodon skull indicates an eight-meter wingspan (Harkson 1966).

Protocrocodilians These small archosaurs tend to be very like protodinosaurs in design: gracile, with fairly erect limbs and digitigrade feet. Certainly their fastest gait was a bounding gallop. The wrist is bizarre because two of the proximal carpals are hyperelongated. Quite unique, this may be a way of lengthening the hand while retaining a plantigrade stance. The outer toe is extremely reduced. The reconstruction by Crush (1983) of *Terrestrisuchus gracilis* is very nice except for the sway back.

Predatory dinosaurs The first dinosaurs such as *Lagosuchus talampayensis* (Fig. 10a) were tiny predators, only a foot or so long and weighing only a tenth of a kilo. The long, flexible backs of these erect, long-limbed animals suggest that they often bounded, but their fore limbs are short enough for bipedal running too. Whether they had a divergent thumb weapon is not known. The outer toe is extremely reduced, and the toe claws are larger than in most thecodonts.

More similar to theropods are *Staurikosaurus, Herrerasaurus* (which is not a juvenile of the former), and other early predatory dinosaurs. Unlike that of true theropods, the ilium remains short and the fourth toe is still fully developed. Very short fore limbs do demonstrate full bipedality. *Herrerasaurus* is unusual in having a retroverted pubis, mimicking protobirds and ornithischians.

Theropods are a uniform group, very bird-like, fully bipedal with short trunks, long, deep narrow hips, and long, narrow, three-toed feet (Figs. 10b–14). Thousands of theropod trackways prove that they always strode, never hopped (contra Raath 1977).

I am amazed by continuing claims that theropods were mere scavengers (Halstead and Halstead 1981). Animals do not go around with 6-inch teeth and enormous jaw muscles just to pick at carcasses! Purely terrestrial scavengers are unknown; only weakly beaked and footed soaring birds can afford the enormous search time required to find dead animals (Houstan 1979). The suggestion by Welles (1984) that slender-snouted *Dilophosaurus*

killed with its feet does not take into account the vomers bracing the snout or the very large teeth. The longstanding belief that theropods were aquaphobic never had any basis. Almost all animals swim well, including big ground birds, and the powerfully limbed, long-toed theropods were probably better at swimming and traversing mud flats than most dinosaurs (see Coombs 1980).

Lips probably covered the teeth when the mouth was closed. Theropod cheeks are broader than the narrow snout. Theropods did not have raptorlike orbital bars shading their eyes. However, their skulls did bear a varying array of crests and horn bosses. The nasal horn of *Ceratosaurus* is well known, *Proceratosaurus* and *Ornitholestes* (Paul, in press, c) had them too. Many other theropods had rugose nasal surfaces that supported a low horn ridge, including ornithomimids. Still others had sharply rimmed and prominent outer nasal edges enlarged by horn ridges. This was taken to an extreme in bony (not horn) crested *Dilophosaurus*. In protobirds the nasal horn sheaths may have migrated forward to form a protobeak. Virtually all theropods and protobirds had a small hornlet or boss just above and before the orbit, sometimes another just above and behind the orbit. In *Carnotaurus* these combined into a hyperenlarged horn (Bonaparte 1985).

Tarsitano (1983) suggests that theropod necks were straight, but so strong is the vertebrae's beveling that it is questionable whether they could completely straighten their necks (Osborn 1906, 1917; Gilmore 1920; Ostrom 1969; Madsen 1976). I show them in their naturally articulated or neutral S curve and the skull extended to its maximum, a rather canidlike threat posture. Normally theropods carried their necks more erect to shift the center of gravity closer to the hind limbs and improve the view of the landscape (Fig. 5). The slender, birdlike neck of small theropods must have been lightly muscled; in big species tall occipital crests imply powerful, bulldog upper-neck muscles. The base of the tail tilted up a little.

Early theropods up to *Ceratosaurus* have four fingers, of which the outer is very reduced and unclawed. Most theropods have three fingers, tyrannosaurs only two (the disarticulated and poorly

Figure 9. "*Quetzalcoatlus northropi* trio" in flapping flight. The head of an adult was about 2 meters long, and its total wingspan was some 11 meters (much of the data for this restoration is from half-sized specimens). This animal apparently had a posterior skull crest, but its form is not known; the individual with larger crest is a "male." Note that fur streamlines the fore-limb bones, muscles, and joints into the leading half of the wings. For AeroVironment version, see MacCready (1985) and Parrish (1986).

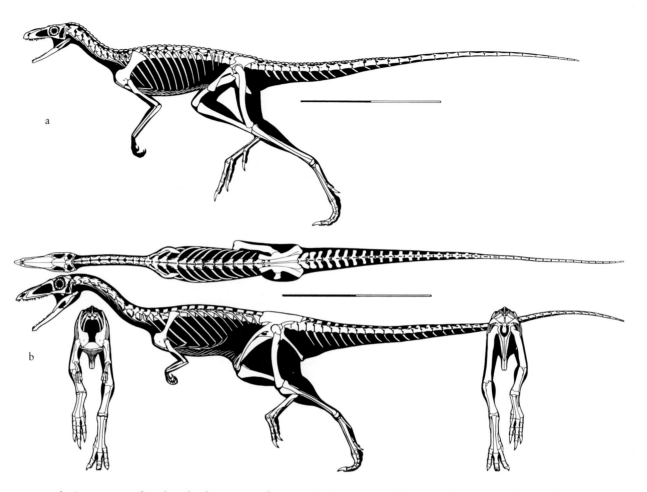

Figure 10. a. *Lagosuchus talampayensis* mainly after PVL 3870. The skull is restored in part after *Lewisuchus,* the hand is unknown; data is from Bonaparte (1971, 1975); scale bar equals 100 millimeters. Note that even this protodinosaur has an S-curved neck. b. The early theropod *Coelophysis (= Syntarsus) rhodesiensis* based primarily on holotype QG 1; scale bar equals 500 millimeters. Compare to Raath (1977), whose restoration is too long in the neck and too short in the trunk.

preserved *Compsognathus* hands do not confirm Ostrom's 1978 suggestion of two fingers).

Tarsitano (1983) argues that theropod hips must have been tilted up twenty degrees when moving, not horizontal. Actually either is possible. We cannot reconstruct and measure limb action and muscle-stretch values well enough to know. The narrow-hipped theropods waddled only a little, like narrow-hipped ground birds, not like fat-hipped ducks. The innermost hind digit is very reduced. That many articulated skeletons show this toe only partly reversed, while some trackways show it fully reversed, suggests that it was mobile. The three central toes, which are long in even the biggest species, are underlain by birdlke rows of small pads and are a little pigeon-toed. The outer digit is reduced to an ankle splint. The toe claws are smaller and blunter in allosaurs, ornithomimids, and tyrannosaurs. Hence they delivered ostrich kicks instead of bouncing on their slender tails.

I find it difficult to conceive of the very

Archaeopteryx-like small theropods not being feathered as are their bird descendants. As for big theropods, Russell (personal communication) has found a small patch of small mosaic scales on the tail of a tyrannosaur. It is quite likely that, like birds, theropods had rows of large scales running along the upper surfaces of the feet and toes. *Ceratosaurus* has an unusual row of irregular scutes running atop its vertebral spines (Gilmore 1920). It is very unlikely that *Tyrannosaurus rex* had scutes (Osborn 1906), all other articulated tyrannosaur skeletons lack them.

It is often stated that juvenile theropods hunted independently, but since many dinosaurs were social it is likely that adult theropods took care of the juveniles, at least until partly grown.

Bidar, Demay, and Tnomel (1972), who postulate that *Compsognathus* was a webbed-handed diver, provide a treatise on how not to describe and illustrate a dinosaur. All tyrannosaurs, not just *rex,* had unusually broad cheeks and a fair

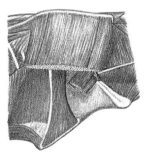

degree of binocular vision, which is sometimes obscured by lateral crushing. The skull cheeks of the well-known *T. rex* at the American Museum of Natural History (AMNH 5027) are too broad due to dorso-ventral crushing, but Molnar (1973) makes them too triangular. Newman (1970) correctly shortened the tail of *T. rex*, but the disarticulated neck vertebrae and drooping foot are in error (see Paul and Chase, in press).

The protobird *Archaeopteryx lithographica* has big, fully aerodynamic, powerfully muscled fore limbs and probably flew well. It lived upon arid islands that supported only scrub (Viohl 1985); the many restorations showing it in trees are, therefore, not correct. It was a good climber, though, and may have been a shorebird that rested in shoreline foliage. Birds do not regularly hunt ultraswift dragonflies, so restorations showing protobirds engaged in such activity are not tenable.

Examination of another protobird, *Velociraptor antirrhopus*, shows that it has much the

Figure 11. The first restoration of the recently mounted, nearly complete *Allosaurus fragilis*, USNM 4734; details of tail are partly from other specimens. This specimen is shorter skulled and more slenderly built than most other allosaurs. The muscle restoration shows it feeding on a carcass, the insert exposes the hip musculature. Scale bar equals 1 meter.

Figure 12. *"Tyrannosaurus (Daspletosaurus) torosus* in a Fast Run." The power of the skull and hind limb are emphasized at the expense of the fore limbs. The locale is a cattail marsh in the Judith River. This painting has been extensively modified (the original version is reproduced in Paul 1984b). Checklist 84.

same large, low head with an upturned snout as *Velociraptor mongoliensis* (Figs. 13–14; Paul, in press, c; Barsbold 1983). These share with *Archaeopteryx* long, highly retroverted pubes that project behind the short ischia and ventral-caudal muscles that connect directly to the pubis as in birds. The restoration of *Saurornithoides* (= *Stenonychosaurus*) *inequalis* by Russell and Seguin (1982) is too broad in the posterior skull (Currie 1985) and too slender in the hips and hind-limb muscles. Barsbold (1983) has shown that *Oviraptor mongoliensis* skulls had a strange nasal prominence.

The ostrich-mimic ornithomimids are usually restored with straight-edged beaks or with a sharply upturned beak tip (Osmolska, Roniewicz, and Barsbold 1972). Actually all ornithomimids share fluted upper beaks with a prominent maxillary flute, a slightly downturned, squared-off tip, and a curved lower beak tip.

Herbivorous dinosaurs Cooper (1980) contends that prosauropod hands were unsuitable for locomotion, but all known prosauropod trackways show these herbivorous dinosaurs walking on all fours (Baird 1980; Olsen and Galton 1984). Pro-

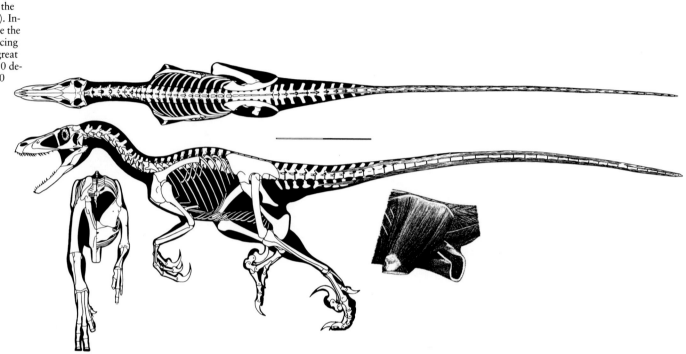

PREVIOUS PAGE
Figure 13. "Resting *Velociraptor antirrhopus* Pair." Most big predators spend most of their time relaxing and sleeping while digesting their last meal. This pair is getting hungry, as shown by their hollow bellies. These protobirds are shown insulated in feathers. Note the various horn ridges on the head and the proto-beak. Only the tips of the teeth show beneath the upper lip. The locale is the Cloverly Formation; the flora consists of ground ferns and the bizarre tree fern *Tempskya,* its fronds blowing in the wind of an oncoming storm. Checklist 83.

sauropods have among the longest and most flexible backs of dinosaurs, and they retained a primitive bounding gallop (Fig. 15). As Bakker (1978) notes, prosauropods probably reared high to browse.

Heavily built, shortfooted prosauropods such as *Euskelosaurus* (= *Melanorosaurus, Riojasaurus)* were the ancestors of sauropods. The more complex vertebral articulations and shorter hind feet suggest that they galloped less and trotted more. Measurements of a *Euskelosaurus* hand and foot by Ellenberger and Ginsberg (1966) must be reversed because as presented the hind feet are absurdly tiny and the hands enormous. Prosauropods have five free fingers, of which only the inner three bear claws. The slightly outward-facing hind feet

are four-toed, each with a large claw and small pads.

Prosauropods were beginning to develop cheeks at the back of their mouths (Paul 1984b). Slender birdlike necks and small skulls suggest light muscles. Galton (1985) shows that prosauropods were herbivores, not predators as suggested by Cooper (1980) and others. It is important to note that all reports of blade toothed prosauropods and sauropods are due to false associations with the shed teeth or fragmentary jaws of truly predatory archosaurs.

Despite the great difficulties in excavating sauropods, a surprising array of new species based on very good skeletons has recently been uncovered on four continents. That their skeletons continue to

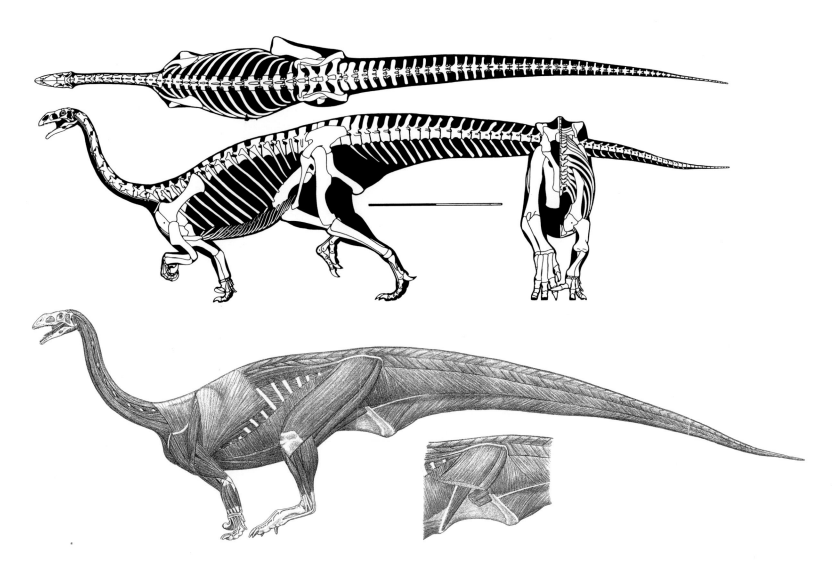

be mounted incorrectly shows that they are in need of a structural reappraisal. Riggs (1904) and Bakker (1971b, c) show that sauropods were terrestrial, a view that appears almost universally accepted (excepting Halstead and Halstead 1981). Indeed they preferred seasonally dry, open conifer-cycadeoid woodlands where they browsed among the tree crowns (Bakker 1971b, c; Dodson, Behrensmeyer, and Bakker 1980). The incompletely straight knee and ankle of the very early *Vulcanodon* suggest that it was a little faster than the others.

Coomb's suggestion (1975) that sauropods had proboscides is unlikely because of the lack of appropriate facial muscles, the absence of scars for these muscles, and the weakness of the nasal bar in some species. Furthermore, sauropod jaws and teeth are well-worn, strong, powerfully muscled cropping organs that did, I believe, not need the assistance of a trunk. Because their mouths were for cropping, not chewing, sauropods lost all traces of cheeks.

Many sauropods had erect, S-curved necks. Diplodocids differ in that the neck was straighter and more horizontal (contra Knight in Massey-Czerkas and Glut 1982: 38, 43; Watson and Zallinger 1960; Bakker in Crompton 1968, and personal communication). Since sauropod skulls were small and the neck vertebrae are very like those of long-necked birds, their necks were lightly muscled. *Brachiosaurus brancai* (Fig. 17) is quite unusual in having withers—tall neural spines over the shoul-

Figure 15. *Plateosaurus engelhardti,* HMN XXV, with skull based on AMNH 6810; data are from Huene (1932). Prosauropods are the only dinosaurs that retain both the clavicle and interclavicle, but they are not connected. The muscle restoration shows the dinosaur in a bounding gallop, the insert exposes the hip musculature. Scale bar equals 1 meter.

ders—that may have supported a set of low cam-ellike nuchal ligaments. Brachiosaurs and many sauropods retain single neural spines, but advanced diplodocids and camarasaurs are famous for their V-shaped neck spines. That a cable ligament lay between these spines is unlikely because it would have had little leverage in this position. Alexander's calculations (1985) that sauropod neck-lifting ligaments and muscles projected well above the neural spines ignore the tissues between and astride the spines. Instead the space between the V spines may have been partly hollow.

The base of all sauropod tail vertebrae articulates in an upward arch (Gilmore 1932, 1936). Lacking any leverage, the whiplash vertebrae of diplodocids must have drooped from the fleshy section of the tail.

Riggs (1904) and Bakker (1971c, 1978) are almost certainly correct in arguing that, like giant ground sloths, diplodocids reared into a tripodal stance to feed or fight. It is the only explanation for their extremely massive hips and associated vertebrae, since other, bigger sauropods have much smaller hips and posterior vertebrae. Rearing also explains the diplodocid's straight necks, short fore limbs, and sledlike chevrons. All sauropods, even *Brachiosaurus*, however, bore most of their mass on their more robust hind limbs and could rear on occasion. Sauropod-theropod combat must have been impressive (Fig. 16).

This is confirmed by the divergent, big-clawed thumb weapons of diplodocids, which are separate from the main united finger unit. Camarasaur and brachiosaur thumbs are not separate and are much smaller. The rest of the hand digits are extraordinarily reduced and short in sauropods; not even hooves were present. Very odd is the rarity of thumb prints in fore prints (Bird 1944, 1985; Lockley, this book) although at least one thumb-claw print is reported by Ginsberg et al. (1966). Some shallow prints can be attributed to diplodocids walking with thumb claws clear of the ground, but not the deep ones.

Sauropod hind limbs, always stouter than their fore limbs, were laterally broad but anteroposteriorly slender compared to those of elephants. The plantigrade hind feet in Cooper's sauropod re-

Figure 16. "Ambush at Como Creek: *Allosaurus atrox* Pack Versus a *Diplodocus carnegii* Herd," an example of what combat between big theropods and sauropods may have been like. Note that the diplodocid herd is retreating onto firm ground as two adults protect a juvenile. Locale is the famous Como Bluff quarry in Wyoming, Morrison Formation. Araucarian and other conifers, cycadioids, and ferns make up the rather dry adapted flora. This painting has been substantially modified (an earlier version is reproduced in Bird [1985] and Czerkas [1986]). Checklist 89.

construction (1984) resulted from a misarticulated astragulus and incomplete tibia. In well-preserved sauropod ankles the astragulus is actually rotated backward relative to that of prosauropods (Janensch 1961: pl. XXI), giving them elephant-style, unguligrade hind feet. They are also rather like African elephants in the absence of hooves on two of the toes; but unlike elephants in that the inner three or four toes bear increasingly massive banana-shaped claws that sweep down and outward (Hatcher 1901; Bird 1944; Ginsberg et al. 1966). Theropods approaching the hips of sauropods were in danger of receiving a nasty kick!

Because they are so reminiscent of elephants it is tempting to restore sauropods with thick, wrinkled skin. Small patches of skin impressions, however, show a thin, unwrinkled skin of very small bead scales, which could not have been seen from more than a few meters away. It appears that a few species may have been lightly armored (Powell 1980), but this is not yet completely certain.

Burian's well-known restoration of *Brachiosaurus brancai* (Spinar and Burian 1972) is faulty in almost all respects, including being posed in an unnatural gorge lake. My new restoration (Paul, in press, b: fig. 24a) shows that *B. brancai* is shorter trunked and more gracile than previously realized. The largest *B. brancai* specimens are similar in size to "Ultrasaurus."

Many of the new Chinese sauropods appear to represent a radiation of basal diplodocids. He et al. (1984) note that *Omeisaurus* and *Mamenchisaurus* are close relatives. Therefore the skull of *Omeisaurus*, instead of the skull of *Diplodocus*, should be used to restore the unknown head of *Mamenchisaurus*. Watson and Zallinger (1960) and Zallinger (1977) persist in restoring *Apatosaurus* with the overly long plaster fore limbs of the AMNH mount (a good example of why one must be sure to determine what is real and not in skeletons!).

I find the elephantine sauropods among the most elegant and majestic of all creatures.

Ornithischians are characterized by beaks, cheeks covering the sides of the mouth (Galton 1973), and retroverted pubes. Horn lengthened the beaks. Tyson (1977) shows that the cheek was probably a pinnate muscle that formed a gentle contour as it rose from under the jugal. Even the most primitive species, including *Lesothosaurus*, had them (Paul 1984a). The ribs tend to bunch closer together at their lower ends than in other dinosaurs. Note that the posterior ribs were always in front of the prepubis, never outside it.

Having beaks, cheeks, and retroverted pubes, segnosaurs can be considered basal ornithopods (Paul 1984a); certainly they are not theropods. No single good specimen exists, so parts from various segnosaurs must be used for a composite restoration (Fig. 18a). *Nanshungisaurus*, published as a small sauropod (Dong 1979), is a segnosaur. Enormous-clawed *Therizanosaurus*, published as a theropod, has a remarkably segnosaurlike scapulacoracoid and humerus. These rather prosauropodlike quadrupeds have four-toed feet with remarkably big claws. The anterior iliac blade flares outward an incredible amount and supports an enormous gut.

The long, strong fore limbs of these early, yet sophisticated and gracile ornithischians suggest that heterodontosaurs were quadrupedal gallopers. The best-articulated skeleton clearly shows a strong downward arch (Fig. 18b; contra Santa-Luca 1980). This skeleton also has inwardly divergent thumbs as per Bakker and Galton (1974), and their restoration of the hand is more accurate than Santa-Luca's. The five-fingered hand bears three inner claws, the four toes a claw each.

Scelidosaurus (Fig. 19a) and *Scutellosaurus* are primitive, quadrupedal ornithischians that lack the skeletal specializations of stegosaurs and ankylosaurs, but have extensive armor coverings. Indeed the body form is so standard that there is little that needs to be said about it. *Scelidosaurus* has normal dinosaur skin (Norman 1985). The hands are not known, the feet have four-clawed toes.

With the anterior dorsal ribs swept back, the shoulder girdle of the stegosaur is set far back, so that they have long, slender, S-curved necks instead of the short, stout, straight one seen in most restorations. The tail base is upwardly arched.

Bakker (1971c, 1978) is probably correct in suggesting that stegosaurs reared to feed, using their surprisingly diplodocidlike tails as a prop. Of

Figure 17. *Brachiosaurus brancai*, HMN SII, with most of posterior column, hips, and hind limbs after other specimens; compare to Janensch (1950a). Note the withers formed by tall shoulder spines—only chasmosaurs (Fig. 23) also have this. Insert exposes the hip musculature.

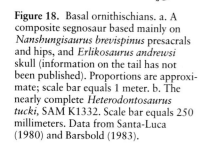

Figure 18. Basal ornithischians. a. A composite segnosaur based mainly on *Nanshungisaurus brevispinus* presacrals and hips, and *Erlikosaurus andrewsi* skull (information on the tail has not been published). Proportions are approximate; scale bar equals 1 meter. b. The nearly complete *Heterodontosaurus tucki,* SAM K1332. Scale bar equals 250 millimeters. Data from Santa-Luca (1980) and Barsbold (1983).

course, their tails were also powerful weapons.

The small, early stegosaur *Huayangosaurus* is only partly rectigrade in limb design, and unlike other stegosaurs it could probably still trot. Stegosaur hands and feet are exceptionally short and small, with only three toes. The digits themselves are exceptionally short. The inner two fingers have flat hooves (Sereno personal communication), the outer three are buried. There are only three toes; these have blunt, vertical, rather elephantlike hooves and were backed by a large elephantine hind pad.

Small armor nodules encase the neck (obviously this slender organ was a tempting target). The great plates and horns were much enlarged by horn sheaths and not skin alone as implied by Buffrenil, Farlow, and de Ricqlès (1984). Bakker (in Wood et al. 1972) suggests that the plates, except the broad-based front and back plates, were mobile. A pair of virtually identical plates in the holotype *Stegosaurus ungulatus* (YPM 1853, Ostrom and McIntosh 1966: pls. 59–1, 60) suggests that

the plates were paired, but other arrangements are possible (Czerkas, this book). In *S. stenops* the s-curved tail tip and differentially beveled spike bases caused the spikes to diverge from each other like a pincushion (Fig. 20b; Ostrom and McIntosh 1966: pl. 54). Some stegosaurs appear to lack this adaptation (Dong, Zhou, and Zhang 1983: fig. 102).

Most stegosaurs are like other ornithischians in being fairly long and low. *Stegosaurus stenops* (Fig. 19b) proves to be about as tall and short as *S. ungulatus*. But Lull's *S. ungulatus* restoration (1910), based on different-sized specimens, is too short. *S. stenops* has exceptionally large plates; *S. ungulatus* has four or more pairs of tail spines to the former's two.

The idea that these very elephantine animals rolled up like hedgehogs for protection (Ratkevich 1976; McLoughlin 1979) is best characterized as ludicrous.

Carpenter (1982, 1984) has done crucial work on the difficult problem of reconstructing the skeletons and armor of ankylosaurs and nodosaurs.

I have not attempted a skeletal reconstruction because of unresolved design question. Coombs (1979, personal communication) and Huene (1956) indicate that ankylosaurs have twenty-four to twenty-six presacral vertebrae, Carpenter and Nopsca (1928) suggest twenty. In addition, some ankylosaur and nodosaur pelves are incredibly broad, and personal inspection revealed no strong dorso-ventral crushing. But other specimens (especially British Museum (Natural History), BMNH 5161) and Carpenter (1984) suggest narrower pelves. It is particularly difficult to resolve the greatly differing lengths of the sacralized dorsal ribs in various specimens and reconstructions.

Ankylosaurs are unusual among dinosaurs in having relatively small eyes. The tail base is directed downward, but the tail does not drag on the ground (Carpenter 1982, 1984). The idea of Wood et al. (1972) that ankylosaurs were made primarily of "solid fat" is due to a misunderstanding about their great girth (Bakker personal communication).

The fusion of a scapulacoracoid to a rib in one specimen (Maryanska 1977) is difficult to confirm. If correct, it is either a pathological or a secondary restriction of scapular mobility. The nodosaur's vertical fore limbs are evidence of a slow gait. The hind-limb-dominant nodosaurs, however, have short fibulas (Coombs 1979: fig. 5d–e) so that the knee appears to have been flexed and the ankle was mobile. This condition is intriguing because it is similar to but the reverse of that seen in fore-limb-dominant camels, which have straight knees and flexed elbows (Muybridge [1887] 1957). Apparently these animals have kept their strongest limbs flexed for trotting and slow galloping. The stronger-limbed, completely flex-jointed ankylosaurs were probably full gallopers. They have five free fingers, of which the inner three or four appear to have had small hooves. Trackways show that the slightly outward facing hind feet were backed by a fairly large, rhinolike pad. The four toes were separate and bore well-developed hooves.

When the body proportions are pinned down, the remains of articulated armor and impressions of skin make these among the most restorable of dinosaurs.

Pachycephalosaurs are among the most bi-zarre of dinosaurs and the only ones more interesting in top view than in side view (Fig. 20). This is because of their incredibly broad ribcages and unbelievably long tail-base transverse processes. No other dinosaur has anything like the latter. The absence of anterior chevrons is another peculiarity. The unusually spacious tail base must have supported an unprecedented migration of part of the digestive tract to behind the hips (Bakker, this book). That the neck is unknown is unfortunate since it may have been specialized to absorb the stress of using the dome-roofed skull as a battering weapon. The tail base is down-arched a little, and its end is stiffened by a crisscross of ossified rods. The hands are unknown, the four-toed hind limbs are like those of ornithopods.

Psittacosaurs are rather like small ornithopods in overall design. Fairly long fore limbs suggest they were at least partly quadrupedal trotters or gallopers. The jugals form very prominent cheek bosses that project out behind the narrow but deep parrot beak. The hand has four small fingers of which the outer is very reduced and the inner three have small blunt hooflets. The foot has four blunt-clawed toes of which the inner is short.

Several researchers (Bakker 1968; Russell 1970b; Coombs 1978) have suggested that proto-ceratopsians ran bipedally. Since scapular rotation makes the fore limbs as long as the hind limbs there is, however, no good reason for dinosaurs with such heavy heads and necks (including *Microceratops*) not to have used them. The fastest gait of the stiff-backed protoceratopsids and the big ceratopsids was probably a fairly smooth, asymmetrical, rhinolike gallop (Fig. 21).

Despite the ceratopsians' very large heads, the hind limbs are the more robust and bear most of the weight. Their trunk is also short, so ceratopsians could rear. After all, horses, bighorn sheep, takin, and elephants rear even though they are fore-limb dominant. Ceratopsians may have reared to reach the occasional choice food item or—like an enraged bear—to present a most intimidating visage to rivals and tyrannosaurs (Fig. 22). It is unlikely that horned dinosaurs relied on defensive rings. This is a specialty of open-tundra musk oxen (Nowak and Paradiso 1983), which spot predators

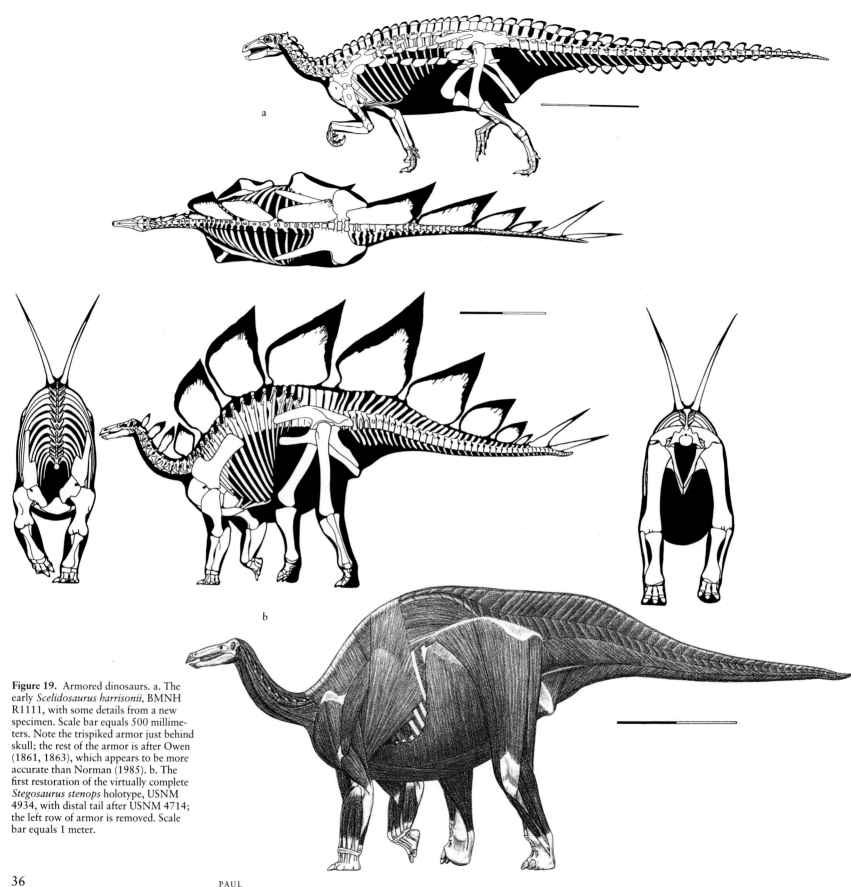

Figure 19. Armored dinosaurs. a. The early *Scelidosaurus harrisonii*, BMNH R1111, with some details from a new specimen. Scale bar equals 500 millimeters. Note the trispiked armor just behind skull; the rest of the armor is after Owen (1861, 1863), which appears to be more accurate than Norman (1985). b. The first restoration of the virtually complete *Stegosaurus stenops* holotype, USNM 4934, with distal tail after USNM 4714; the left row of armor is removed. Scale bar equals 1 meter.

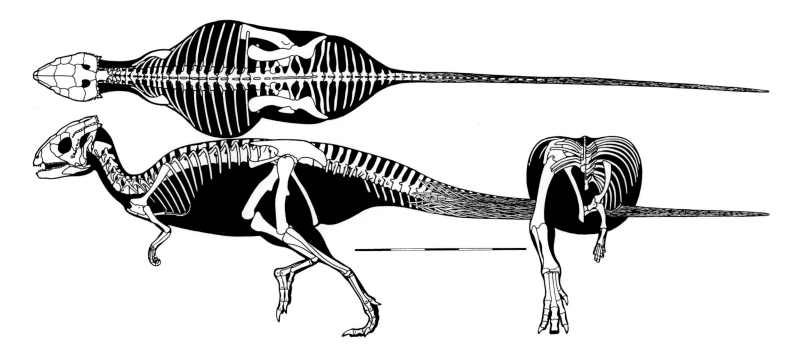

at great distances. Ceratopsians lived in wooded habitats (Russell 1977) that may have prevented them from organizing defensive rings. Their best defense was probably aggressive charging or flight into dense bush.

The restoration of the styracosaur beak by Spinar and Burian (1972), which is much too broad, has been faithfully copied by many other artists! An array of hornlets and bosses decorates the frill rim, midline, squamosal upper surface, jugal tip, and sometimes the area in front of the nasal horn. Care should be taken to apply the proper number of these elements in each species. Horn undoubtedly emphasized their appearance in life (Figs. 1, 21–23), especially in styracosaurs. In ungulates horn sheaths add from a third to double the length of the bone core; a middle value is best used for ceratopsian horns.

Rowe, Colbert, and Nations (1981) show the actual shape of the *Chasmosaurus (Pentaceratops) sternbergi* frill, and *C. russeli* has a similar frill (Sternberg 1940). It has long been argued that the frill anchored the great closing muscles of the jaw. This is the only good explanation for the great bone structure (see Fig. 1). All other big-headed animals lack such a structure, so it was not needed to

counterbalance the skull as Tyson argues (1977). Display could be handled by soft tissues, so this was only a secondary function (Pringle 1978: cover). Finally in some chameleon specimens the surfaces of the frill bearing the jaw muscle are highly channeled as in ceratopsids (contra Tyson [1977]). If the suprafenestral horns of *Monoclonius* and *Anchiceratops* are the ossified cartilagenous spurs of a pinnate frill muscle they indicate that the muscle was a fairly robust belly instead of a thin sheet. Ceratopsids had wickedly powerful bites, and short-horned chasmosaurs probably bit at predators like the big-incisored Asian rhinos.

The head articulates with the neck via a highly mobile ball-and-socket joint. The neck is gently curved upward, not straight as per Lull (1933). Because the anterior dorsal ribs are swept back and the shoulder girdle is set aft, the neck is longer than usually shown. Tyson (1977) shows that the neck muscles attached to the braincase in the normal manner, not to the top of the frill as in Ratkevich (1976) and McLoughlin (1979). Hip and tail orientation is very variable, with the tail eventually directed downward (Fig. 23). The posterior dorsal ribs are strongly curved fore and aft (specimens seeming to show otherwise are partly

Figure 20. The first modern restoration of a "domehead," *Homocephale calathocercos* holotype, GI 100/51, with the neck restored and fore limbs and some other details after *Stegoceras*. The anterior caudals with their hyperelongated transverse processes are included in the posterior view. Data in part from Maryanska and Osmolska (1974). Scale bar equals 500 millimeters.

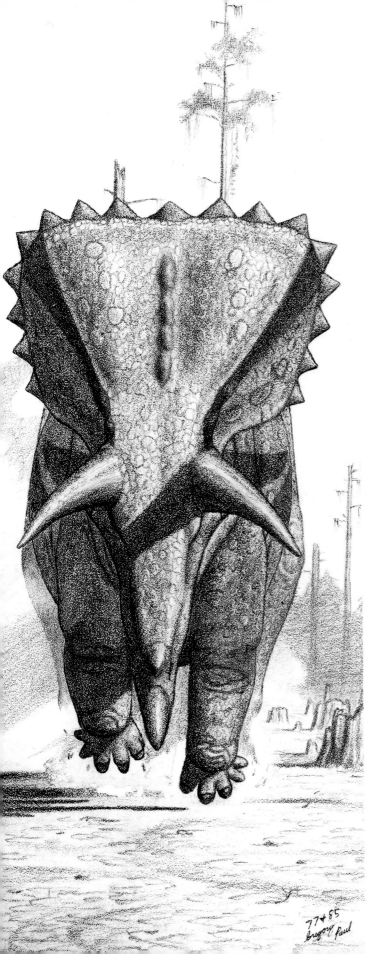

disarticulated), and one of these ribs was connected in life to the tip of the prepubis (Fig. 23; Osborn 1933).

The five fingers and four toes of protoceratopsids and ceratopsids are all free, finger 5 and toe 1 are much shorter than the others. The fingers and toes bear fairly large, flat hooves, except as usual the hoofless outer two fingers. The hind feet were probably backed by a fairly large, rhinolike pad.

Although rhinolike in body form, large skin patches show that ceratopsid skin is a very "reptilian" mosaic of large polygonal scales surrounding even larger polygonal scales (B. Brown 1917; Lull 1933). Combined with the horns, hornlets, and bosses, these large scales presented a very rich topography (Bakker in Crompton 1968; Figs. 1, 21–23). Unconfirmed is a possible row of scutes atop the tail (B. Brown 1917).

Both the largest and most uniform of the ornithischian groups, ornithopods are very important because some species can be restored with exceptionally high accuracy.

Ornithopods, except hadrosaurs, have orbital bars above the eyes that gave these most unfierce of herbivores threatening "eagle eyes." The bar is fixed to the postorbital in some species, and so it was immobile.

Many ornithopods have normally arched backs. Hadrosaurs, *Ouranosaurus, Tenontosaurus,* and *Othnielia (= Yandusaurus?)*, however, have very strongly down-arched anterior dorsal columns (Figs. 24–26; Bakker 1978; Maryanska and Osmolska 1984). Almost all specimens are preserved this way, and straightening the back violates the anatomy. Straight-backed ornithopods were probably medium-level browsers. The down-arched backs of other ornithopods suggest a preference for browsing ground cover, and this is confirmed by their broader, more rectangular beaks (Figs. 24, 26).

In most ornithopods the tail droops immediately behind the hips (Gilmore 1909; Galton 1970). In iguanodonts and hadrosaurs the tail base is arched up just a little. In most small ornithopods the end of the tail is stiffened by ossified rods; in iguanodonts and hadrosaurs almost the entire post-cervical column is greatly stiffened by ossified rods

Figure 22. "Rearing *Chasmosaurus ?belli."* Rearing may have been an intimidating threat posture of ceratopsids; the object of this animal's attentions may be another member of the species or a predator. The rich skin topography is restored after skin impressions. Locale is a bald cypress lake with water lily and duckweed type plants in the Judith River Formation; the moon is about to occult Venus.

OPPOSITE
Figure 21. "Charging *Triceratops horridus* group." Even the biggest of the ceratopsians were built for rhinolike galloping. Fore-limb action is shown a little too erect (see Fig. 23b). Locale is a dried-out bald cypress swamp in the Lance-Hell Creek Formation. This painting has been substantially revised (for original version see Gould [1978, 1980]). Checklist 70.

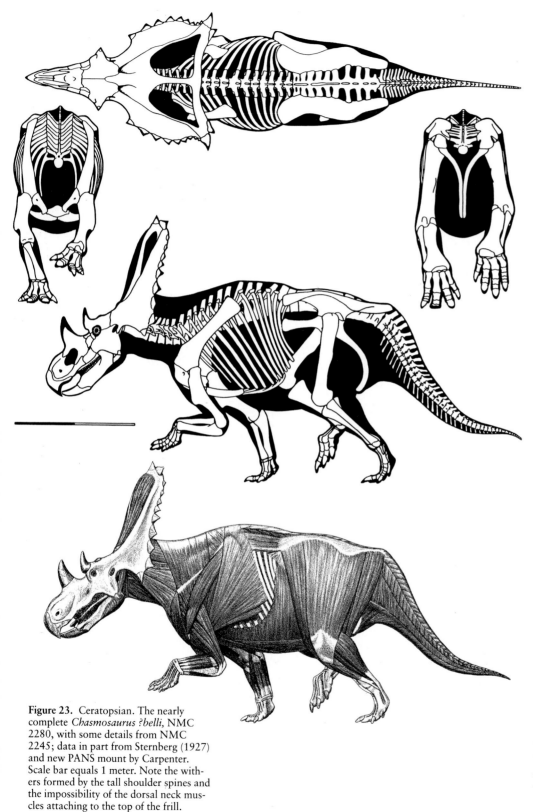

Figure 23. Ceratopsian. The nearly complete *Chasmosaurus ?belli*, NMC 2280, with some details from NMC 2245; data in part from Sternberg (1927) and new PANS mount by Carpenter. Scale bar equals 1 meter. Note the withers formed by the tall shoulder spines and the impossibility of the dorsal neck muscles attaching to the top of the frill.

and restrictive articulations. Although all ornithopods could rear (Maryanska and Osmolska 1984) to high browse, display, or in the case of camptosaurs and iguanodonts fight, the many restorations that show iguanodonts and hadrosaurs resting kangaroo-style on bent tails are incorrect.

In most small ornithopods and camptosaurs the fore limbs are too short to use at any but the slowest speeds. In *Tenontosaurus, Muttaburrasaurus,* iguanodonts, and hadrosaurs the fore limbs are long-running organs, and trackways prove that the fore limbs were used at least occasionally (Norman 1980; Currie 1983). The common trackways showing only hind prints do not prove that they were walking bipedally because the hind feet may have wiped out the fore prints. The fastest gait of this long-fore-limbed species was probably a trot as the fore limbs are too slender to support a gallop. In most preiguanodonts the five fingers are free and bear hooves on the inner three. The four long toes are also free and ·underlain by small individual pads. Trackways and a recently discovered mummified hand (Currie personal communication) show that the iguanodont's and hadrosaur's three central fingers and hooves are encased in a single hooflike sheath. This is not a web as often thought, nor is digit II in a separate lobe as suggested by the damaged SM R.4306 (contra Bakker this book). The thumb is a great spike weapon in *Camptosaurus, Muttaburrasaurus* (Molnar 1982), and primitive iguanodonts; it dwindles in advanced iguanodonts and is lost in hadrosaurs. The outer digit is free and unhooved. As for the hind feet, trackways and mummies show the three short toes each underlain by a single diamond-shaped pad, backed by a fairly large central pad. The pigeon-toeing seen in ornithopod trackways is not due to bipedal waddling because it persists when the fore prints are present.

Small mosaic scales are known on hadrosaurs, iguanodonts, and tenontosaurs. The hadrosaur "mummies" are both extraordinary and underappreciated for the nearly complete information they provide on surface topography. They invariably show a frill running along most if not all the vertebral column. The frills are continuous skin ribbons in *Edmontosaurus* (Osborn 1912; Horner 1984) and *Hypacrosaurus* (Fig. 25; B. Brown

1916) or made of individual hornlets as in *Krito-saurus* (Parks 1920). The *Edmontosaurus* frill has rectangular dorsal serrations. The *Hypacrosaurus* frill is very deep over the neck and attaches to the crest, as it may have done in all crested hadrosaurs. Small, nonbony hornlets are found on the flanks or belly of some hadrosaurs (B. Brown 1916; Parks 1920). Vertical wrinkles mark some of the ribbon frills and other areas of the body. Most prominent of these are the large vertical skin folds enwrapping the neck base, shoulder, and upper arm. These are not artifacts caused by dessication because they are always present, always vertical, and never found elsewhere on the body. Yet most restorations ignore the dorsal frills, and almost all ignore the shoulder folds.

Some duckbills were giants of twelve to twenty or more metric tons (*Shantungosaurus,* Mesaverde tracks). Only sauropods were bigger.

Virtually complete mummies make *Edmontosaurus annectens* and *Hypacrosaurus casuarius* the two most restorable published dinosaurs. The life restoration of the latter in Figure 25 is estimated to be eighty-five to ninety percent accurate.

The Science of Paleorestoration

Some paleontologists continue to consider paleorestoration as inherently unimportant and impractical. Actually we can no more observe how a living dinosaur population evolves than we can see their appearance. But as astronomers sample stars through their spectra, we can use indirect means to obtain information regarding the appearance of dinosaurs. In some cases dinosaurs can be restored with remarkably high fidelity, almost as accurately as some recently extinct animals. As for the importance of paleorestoration, it is just as interesting to know what a dinosaur looked like as it is to know its relationships. Proper restoration of the design of animals can be important toward understanding their function and ecology.

This paper is intended to reduce the frustrating number of mistakes plaguing the field. These errors cannot all be attributed to a lack of knowledge. Correct information has often been available for decades—the famous, yet underused *Edmontosaurus* mummy was published before

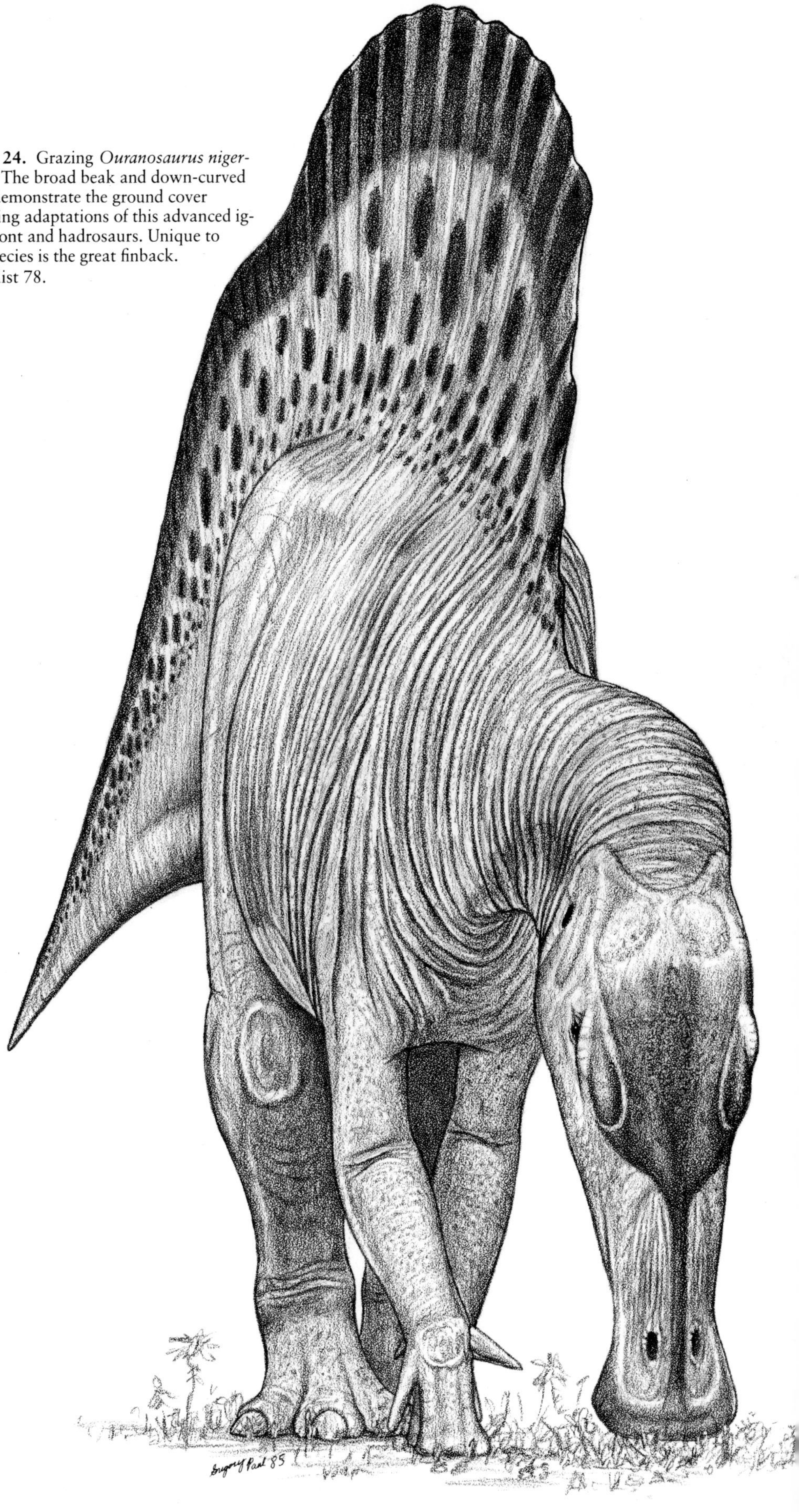

Figure 24. Grazing *Ouranosaurus nigeriensis*. The broad beak and down-curved back demonstrate the ground cover browsing adaptations of this advanced iguanodont and hadrosaurs. Unique to this species is the great finback. Checklist 78.

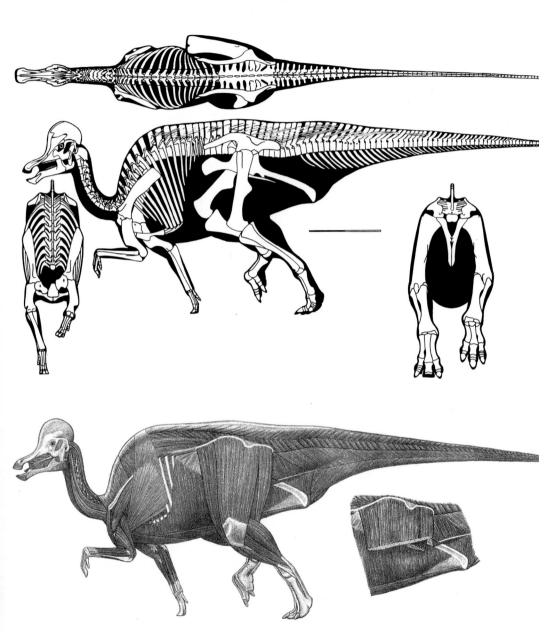

Figure 25. The duck-billed *Hypacrosaurus (= Corythosaurus) casuarius* holotype, AMNH 5240, a nearly complete male mummy in which much of the shown skin topography is preserved. Scale bar equals 1 meter; insert exposes the hip musculature. Fore limb after AMNH 5338; data from B. Brown (1916).

World War I. In part the problem stems from the postdepression doldrums that long afflicted dinosaurology. The field has revived since the mid-1960s, and dinosaur restoration has not only benefited from but contributed to this revival. Yet the skepticism and the noncritical attitude of some scientists, exhibits personnel, and editors hold it back.

Part of the solution is a more rigorous, critical attitude. The common assertion that there is always more than one way to restore a given animal is not true. Another problem is lavishly detailed restorations that do not capture the basic shape and form of the subject. It is more important to execute the distinctive profile of each dinosaur than to meticulously add hypothetical details. A different problem arises when fine wildlife artists produce cartoonlike renderings (notable exceptions are Kish's work [Russell 1977] and Bill Berry's Dinosaur National Monument restorations [White 1967]). More critical guidance is needed. Further, there must be solid reasons for alternative representations. Herbivorous dinosaurs should not be restored with hollow bellies when this violates all that is known about herbivore alimentary tracts. Hadrosaurs should always be restored with frills and vertical shoulder folds. And tails are best put where they belong, in the air.

Indeed, arching the sauropod's tails over the visitor's head brings us to another point. We need to be daring and bold. Not only are traditional concepts of dinosaur appearance no more intrinsically valid than controversial ones, more often than not they are incorrect. The reasons for illustrating alternative views of dinosaurs are excellent if not imperative.

THE ART

As well as being scientific, the best dinosaur restorations should also be artistic. Most dinosaur restorations are illustrations and do not possess that indefinable air that qualifies them as art. In this regard I disagree with photographic-image restorations. Extinct animals cannot be restored with complete confidence or be photographed. Art is the use of visual cues and creative license to convince people that they are seeing a version of reality.

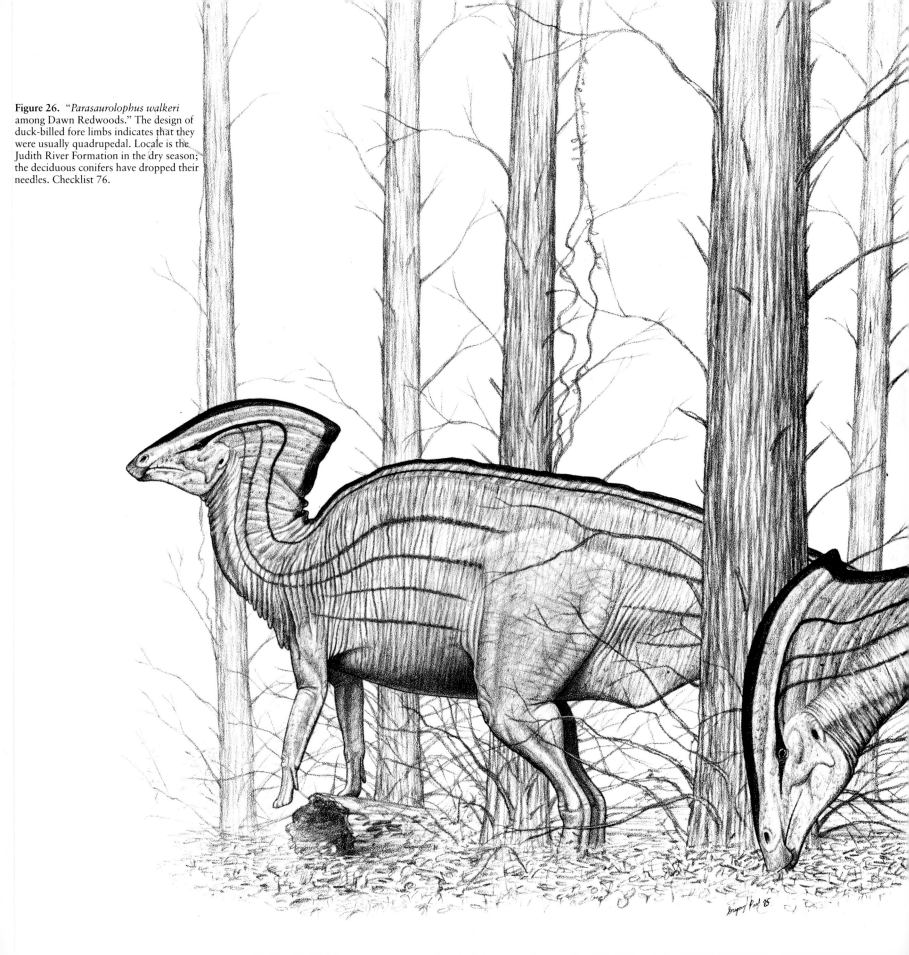

Figure 26. "*Parasaurolophus walkeri* among Dawn Redwoods." The design of duck-billed fore limbs indicates that they were usually quadrupedal. Locale is the Judith River Formation in the dry season; the deciduous conifers have dropped their needles. Checklist 76.

Ewer, R. F. 1965. The anatomy of the thecodont reptile *Euparkeria capensis* Broom. *Philosophical Transactions of the Royal Society of London* B248:379–435.

Farlow, J. O. 1981. Estimates of dinosaur speeds from a new trackway site in Texas. *Nature* 294: 747–48.

Feduccia, A. 1980. *The age of birds.* Cambridge, Mass.: Harvard University Press.

Fürbringer, M. 1876. Zur vergleichenden Anatomie der Schultermuskeln, III. *Morphol. Jahrbuch* 1: 636–816.

Galton, P. M. 1970. The posture of hadrosaurian dinosaurs. *Journal of Paleontology* 44: 464–73.

———. 1971a. Manus movements of the coelurisaurian dinosaur *Syntarsus* and opposability of the theropod hallux. *Arnoldia* 5: 1–8.

———. 1971b. The prosauropod dinosaur *Ammosaurus,* the crocodile *Protosuchus,* and their bearing on the age of the Navajo Sandstone of northern Arizona. *Palaeontologica* 45: 781–95.

———. 1973. The cheeks of ornithischian dinosaurs. *Lethaia* 6: 67–89.

———. 1974. The ornithischian dinosaur *Hysilophodon* from the Wealden of the Isle of Wight. *British Museum of Natural History Bulletin* 25: 1–152.

———. 1985. Diet of prosauropod dinosaurs from the late Triassic and early Jurassic. *Lethaia* 18: 105–23.

George, J. C., and A. J. Berger, 1966. *Avian myology.* New York: Academic Press.

Gilmore, C. W. 1905. A mounted skeleton of *Triceratops. Proceedings of the United States National Museum* 29: 433–35.

———. 1909. Osteology of the Jurassic reptile *Camptosaurus,* with a review of the species and genus, and description of two new species. *Proceedings of the United States National Museum* 36: 197–332.

———. 1915. Osteology of *Thescelosaurus:* An ornithopodous dinosaur from the Lance Formation of Wyoming. *Proceedings of the United States National Museum* 49: 591–616.

———. 1920. Osteology of the carnivorous Dinosauria in the United States National Museum, with special reference to the genera *Antrodemus (Allosaurus)* and *Ceratosaurus. Bulletin of the United States National Museum* 35: 351–66.

———. 1932. On a newly mounted skeleton of *Diplodocus* in the United States National Museum. *Proceedings of the United States National Museum* 81: 1–21.

———. 1936. Osteology of *Apatosaurus,* with special reference to specimens in the Carnegie Museum. *Memoirs of the Carnegie Museum* 11: 175–297.

Ginsberg, L., A. F. Lapparent, B. Loiret, and P. Taquet. 1966. Empreintes de pas de vertebres tetrapodes dans les series continentales a l'Ouest d'Agades (République du Niger). *C. R. Académie Sci. Paris* 263: 28–31.

Glut, D. 1982. *The new dinosaur dictionary.* Secaucus, N.J.: Citadel.

Gould, S. J. 1978. Were dinosaurs dumb? *Natural History* 87, no. 5: 9–16.

———. 1980. *The panda's thumb.* New York: W. W. Norton & Company.

Guggisberg, C. A. 1966. *S.O.S. Rhino.* New York: October House.

Halstead, L. B., and J. Halstead. 1981. *Dinosaurs.* Dorset, England: Blanford.

Harkson, J. C. 1966. *Pteranodon sternbergi:* A new pterodactyl from the Niobrara Cretaceous of Kansas. *Proceedings of the South Dakota Academy of Science* 45: 74–77.

Hatcher, J. B. 1901. *Diplodocus* Marsh: Its osteology, taxonomy and probable habits, with a restoration of the skeleton. *Memoirs of the Carnegie Museum* 1: 1–63.

Haubold, H. 1971. Ichnia amphibiorum et reptiliorum fossilium. *Handbuch der Palaoherpetologie* 10: 1–123.

He X., Li K., Cai K., and Gao Y. 1984. *Omeisaurus tianfuensis:* A new species of *Omeisaurus* from Dashanpu, Zigong, Sichuan. *Journal of Chengdu Coll. Geol.,* supp. 2: 31–44.

Heerden, J. van. 1979. The morphology and taxonomy of *Euskelosaurus* (Reptilia: Saurischia; Late Triassic) from South Africa. *Nav. Nas. Mus.* 4: 21–84.

Heglund, N. C., G. A. Cavagnaga, and C. R. Taylor. 1982. Energetics and mechanics of terrestrial locomotion. *Journal of Experimental Biology* 79: 41–56.

Horner, J. R. 1984. A "segmented" epidermal tail frill in a species of hadrosaurian dinosaur. *Journal of Paleontology* 58: 270–71.

Hotton, N. 1980. An alternative to dinosaur endothermy: The happy wanderers. In *A cold look at the warm-blooded dinosaurs,* ed. D. K. Thomas and E. C. Olson, 311–50. Washington, D.C.: AAAS.

Houstan, D. C. 1979. The adaptations of scavengers. In *Dynamics of an ecosystem,* ed. A. R. E. Sinclair and M. Norton-Griffiths, 263–86. Chicago: University of Chicago Press.

Hu C. 1973. A new hadrosaur from the Cretaceous of Chucheng, Shantung. *Acta Geol. Sinica* 2: 179–206.

Huene, F. R. von. 1932. Die fossile reptil-ordung Saurischia, ihre entwicklung und geschichte. *Mono. Geol. Palaeont.* 4: 1–361.

———. 1956. *Palaeontologie und phylogenie der Niederen Tetrapoden.* Jena, East Germany: Gustav Fisher Verlag.

Janensch, W. 1950a. Die wirbelsäule von *Brachiosaurus brancai. Palaeontographica,* supp. 7, no. 3: 27–93.

———. 1950b. Die skelettrekonstruktion von *Brachiosaurus brancai. Palaeontographica,* supp. 7, no. 3: 97–102.

———. 1961. Die gliedmassen und gliedmassengürtel der sauropoden der Tendaguru-Schichten. *Palaeontographica,* supp. 7, no. 3: 177–235.

Knight, C. R. 1947. *Animal drawing: Anatomy and action for artists.* New York: McGraw-Hill.

Lindstedt, S. L., H. Hoppler, K. M. Bard, and H. A. Thronson. 1987. Estimate of muscle-shortening rate during locomotion. *American Journal of Physiology* 249: R699–R703.

Lockley, M. G., B. H. Young, and K. Carpenter. 1983. Hadrosaur locomotion and herding behaviour: Evidence from footprints in the Mesaverde Formation, Grand Mesa Coal Field, Colorado. *Mountain Geologist* 20: 5–14.

Lull, R. S. 1910. *Stegosaurus ungulatus* Marsh, recently mounted at the Peabody Museum of Yale University. *American Journal of Science* 4, no. 30: 361–78.

———. 1933. A revision of the Ceratopsia, or horned dinosaurs. *Memoirs of the Peabody Museum of Yale University* 3, no. 3: 1–135.

MacCready, P. 1985. The great pterodactyl project. *Engineering and Science* 49: 18–24.

Madsen, J. H. 1976. *Allosaurus fragilis:* A revised osteology. *Utah Geological and Mineralogical Survey Bulletin* 109: 1–163.

Martin, L. D. 1984. The origin of birds and of avian flight. In *Current ornithology,* ed. R. J. Johnston, 105–29. London: Plenum.

Marx, J. L. 1978. Warm-blooded dinosaurs: Evidence pro and con. *Science* 199: 1424–26.

Maryanska, T. 1977. Ankylosauridae (Dinosauria) from Mongolia. *Palaeont. Polonica* 37: 85–151.

Maryanska, T., and H. Osmolska. 1974. Pachycephalosauria, a new suborder of ornithischian dinosaurs. *Palaeont. Polonica* 30: 45–101.

———. 1984. Postcranial anatomy of *Saurolophus angustirostris* with comments on other hadrosaurs. *Palaeont. Polonica* 46: 119–41.

Massey-Czerkas, S., and D. Glut. 1982. *Dinosaurs, mammoths, and cavemen: The art of Charles Knight.* New York: Dutton.

Matsukawa M., and Obata I. 1985. Dinosaur footprints and other indentations in the Cretaceous Sebayashi Formation, Sebayashi. *Japan. Bulletin of the Natn. Sci. Mus.* c11: 9–36.

McGowen, C. 1979. The hindlimb musculature of the Brown Kiwi, *Apteryx australis mantelli. Journal of Morphology* 160: 33–74.

———. 1982. The wing musculature of the Brown Kiwi *Apteryx australis mantelli* and its bearing on ratite affinities. *Journal of Zoology* 197: 179–219.

McLoughlin, J. C. 1979. *Archosauria: A new look at the old dinosaur.* New York: Viking.

McMahon, T. A. 1984. *Muscles, reflexes, and locomotion.* Princeton: Princeton University Press.

Molnar, R. E. 1973. The cranial morphology and mechanics of *Tyrannosaurus rex* (Reptilia: Saurischia). Ph.D. diss., University of California, Los Angeles.

———. 1982. Australian Mesozoic reptiles. In *The fossil vertebrate record of Australia, Melbourne,* ed. P. V. Rich and E. M. Thompson. Melbourne: Monash University Press.

Muybridge, E. [1887] 1975. *Animals in motion,* ed. L. S. Brown. Reprint. New York: Dover.

Newman, B. H. 1970. Stance and gait in the flesh-eating dinosaur *Tyrannosaurus. Biological Journal of the Linnean Society* 2: 119–23.

Nicholls, E. L., and A. P. Russell. 1985. Structure and function of the pectoral girdle and forelimb of *Struthiomimus altus* (Theropoda: Ornithomimidae). *Palaeontology* 28: 643–77.

Norman, D. B. 1980. On the ornithischian dinosaur *Iguanodon bernissartensis* of Bernissart (Belgium). *Memoirs of the Royal Institute of Natural Science, Belgium* 178: 1–103.

———. 1985. *The illustrated encyclopedia of dinosaurs.* New York: Crescent.

Nowak, R. M., and J. L. Paradiso. 1983. *Walker's mammals of the world.* 4th ed. Baltimore: Johns Hopkins University Press.

Olsen, P. E., and P. M. Galton. 1984. A review of the reptile and amphibian assemblages from the Stormberg of southern Africa, with special emphasis on the footprints and the age of the Stormberg. *Palaeont. Afr.* 25: 87–110.

Olshevsky, G. 1981. Dinosaur renaissance. *Science Digest* 89: 34–43.

Osborn, H. F. 1906. *Tyrannosaurus:* Upper Cretaceous carnivorous dinosaur (second communication). *Bulletin of the American Museum of Natural History* 22: 281–97.

———. 1912. Integument of the iguanodont dinosaur *Trachodon. American Museum of Natural History Memoirs* 1: 33–54.

———. 1917. Skeletal adaptations of *Ornitholestes, Struthiomimus, Tyrannosaurus. Bulletin of the American Museum of Natural History* 35: 733–71.

———. 1933. Mounted skeleton of *Triceratops elatus. American Museum Novitates* 654: 1–14.

ECOLOGIC AND BEHAVIORAL IMPLICATIONS DERIVED FROM A DINOSAUR NESTING SITE

JOHN R. HORNER

The Upper Cretaceous Two Medicine Formation dinosaur nesting localities known as Egg Mountain and Egg Island are interpreted using available geologic and paleontologic data. Both sites were small islands located near the shore of a shallow, intermittent, alkaline lake. The climate was seasonally dry with apparent monsoonlike conditions during summer months. Two species of dinosaurs nested repeatedly over a number of years on the islands. Colonial nesting prevailed for both species. Carefully laid-out spiral clutches, derived from a fabrosaurid-like hypsilophodont, and equally carefully arranged linearly oriented eggs of an unknown species suggest female manipulation after egg laying. The hypsilophodont hatchlings appear to have left their respective nests immediately after they were hatched. The young may have remained in the immediate area of the nesting grounds until they reached about half adult size. The presence of a small carnivorous dinosaur, two mammal species, a varanid lizard, and scavenger insects or beetles suggests numerous possible symbiotic relationships between eggs and young and predators.

Localities producing abundant dinosaur remains are found throughout much of the world, but very few of the sites yield the kind of information useful for reconstructing specific habitats and generalized behavior. To make interpretations of these kinds it is necessary that the fossil remains not have been transported. Because dinosaurs were terrestrial animals and lived and died in areas of fluvial deposition, it is very difficult if not impossible in most instances to determine whether or not a fossil specimen is anywhere near its original habitat area. Traces such as footprints and nests are, however, the kinds of dinosaur remains that could not have been transported without destruction. Additionally they are the types of remains from which both habitat and behavior can be interpreted (even if only for a short period of time in the life of the animal).

In the Upper Cretaceous Two Medicine Formation of western Montana numerous dinosaur nesting sites have been located, excavated, and studied (Horner and Makela 1979; Horner 1982a, 1984a, b). Two of these sites, which appear to have been inhabited at the same time, provide habitat and behavior data not previously available from other sites in the world. The two sites, referred to as Egg Mountain and Egg Island, located fifteen kilometers west of Choteau, Teton County, Montana, have yielded abundant egg clutches of two dinosaur species, eggs with embryonic remains, articulated juvenile and adult skeletons of dinosaurs, lizards, and mammals, and invertebrates. None of the specimens appears to have been disturbed other than by contemporaneous bioturbation within the sediments.

Although interpretive scenarios concerning life on Egg Mountain and Egg Island have appeared previously (Horner 1982a, 1984a), little of the original data has been published. In this paper I intend to present all of the information that has to date been derived from the sites and to illustrate some of the inferred habitat and behavioral information.

During the summer of 1979 a crew of thirteen volunteers, directed by me (I was then at Princeton University), were exploring the area in and around Willow Creek Anticline where a nest of hadrosaur babies had been excavated during the previous year. Within the first two weeks the crew had discovered a second hadrosaur nest containing babies, five hadrosaur nests containing eggshell fragments, three hadrosaur skeletons, and an extensive hadrosaur bone bed. On July 10, while excavating one of the hadrosaur skeletons, the crew was interrupted by a group of people and vehicles tracing out a seismic line for oil exploration. The seismic party stated that they would soon be drilling, blasting, and pounding the ground with large machines to record seismic data. Because of the imminent surface destruction that would occur along the seismic line our crew members were sent out to search for specimens that might potentially be destroyed. On July 11 Fran Tannenbaum, an undergraduate at Princeton, discovered a complete egg in a limestone outcropping within inches of a location the seismologists had planned to blast. The remainder of the crew was brought to the site, and before the day was over a clutch of four additional eggs, a dozen partial eggs, hundreds of eggshell fragments, and numerous small bones had been collected. The scientific importance of the site was explained to the seismologists, and they agreed to offset their line around the location. "Frantastic," as the site was originally named, was a small nondescript hill covered with grass, brown limestone boulders, and abundant dinosaur egg and skeletal remains. During the following week Frantastic was mapped and gridded. Then, grid by grid, the crew dry-screened eggshell and bone fragments from the weathered soil. All of the overlying soil was removed from 350 square meters of surface area, and the strata were brushed and washed for additional exposure of in-place specimens. By the end of the 1979 field season a total of fifty-two eggs (twenty-eight in four clutches), a partially articulated varanid lizard skeleton, hundreds of small hypsilophodont dinosaur skeletal remains, and thousands of eggshell fragments had been collected.

Surface collection continued through the field seasons of 1980 and 1981 resulting in an additional sixty-one eggs (fifty-four eggs in clutches), five partial hypsilophodont skeletons, and a partial lizard skeleton. By the end of the 1981 field season it was evident that the clutches of eggs and hypsilophodont skeletons were coming primarily from three stratigraphic horizons and by excavation of any one of the horizons more specimens would be found. In 1982 Bob Makela and a crew of six volunteers began the first excavation, jackhammering straight down from the top of the hill. The excavation site measured approximately eighty-five square meters. The uppermost nesting horizon was reached after three weeks of work and the removal of about fifty tons of rock. So that the overburden would not be transported twice, large wooden

slides were constructed to move the rock down to the bottom of the hill. Because the slope was not particularly steep, crew members had to climb onto the ramps and shove the material down. The crew referred to this task as "skiing Egg Mountain," thus the site's new name was coined. Three badly weathered hypsilophodont clutches were found on the nesting horizon.

As excavation continued the unweathered rock became too difficult to split with the small jackhammers, and the chances of destroying nests became greater. Near the end of the 1982 season vertical excavation was halted, and terrace excavations around the perimeters of the hill were initiated. These excavations yielded a hypsilophodont skeleton, an egg clutch, and an articulated varanid skeleton, all from the middle nesting horizon.

In 1983 a larger jackhammer was acquired for a horizontal excavation straight back into Egg Mountain with a base level below the lowest nesting horizon. At the end of the 1984 season and culmination of work on Egg Mountain more than two hundred metric tons of rock had been removed (Fig. 1). The two-year excavation yielded three hypsilophodont clutches (all from the lowest horizon), four unidentified eggs (one containing an embry-

onic skeleton), an articulated hypsilophodont skeleton, and hundreds of cranial and postcranial elements of hypsilophodonts, mammals, and lizards.

Egg Island, the second hypsilophodont nesting area, was discovered on the last day of the 1983 field season. Although the site was never excavated, surface collecting produced three hypsilophodont clutches, one of which consisted of nineteen eggs each containing an embryonic skeleton.

Egg Mountain (Fig. 2) rises about 20 meters above the surrounding topography. The fossil-bearing units are concentrated within the top 5.6 meters, and the three nesting horizons occur within the uppermost 3 meters (Fig. 3). Egg Island, located about one kilometer from Egg Mountain, rises about 10 meters from the surrounding land and is capped by a 1-meter thick egg-producing horizon. The strata of both sites are nearly flat lying, structurally located on a monocline off the western limb of the Willow Creek Anticline.

Lorenz and Gavin (1984) described the egg-bearing sediments of Egg Mountain and Egg Island as bioturbated, gray calcareous siltstones (Fig. 4a). Gray calcareous mudstones occur between the nesting horizons (Lorenz 1981). X-ray analysis and granular point counts of the calcareous siltstones in

Figure 1. West face of Egg Mountain during the 1984 summer excavation.

Figure 2. Egg Mountain from the north during 1984 summer excavation. Note Rocky Mountains on right.

Figure 3. Three-dimensional map showing relationship of nests on Egg Mountain. Black figures are eggs of unknown origin. Egg clutches represent hypsilophodont nests. Shaded area is either missing or covered. Vertical expression is 3 meters. Sediment block on right shows relationship of calcareous siltstones (even brick pattern) and calcareous mudstones (uneven bricks). After Horner (1984a).

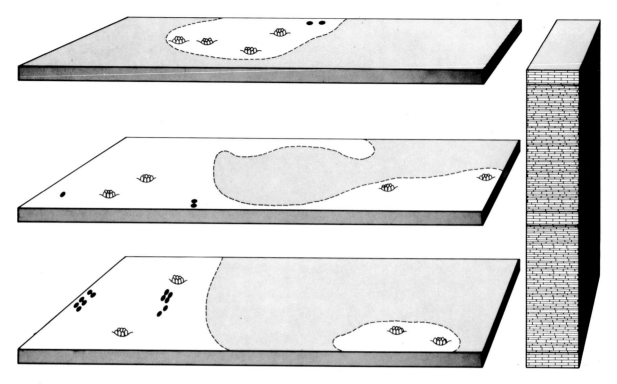

and around individual eggs and adjacent to nests indicate no appreciable differences in sediment composition, and therefore no indication of nest boundaries. The absence of bedding planes and occurrence of suspended sand grains, nonoriented mud chips, pebbles, plant fragments, and skeletal elements suggest considerable bioturbation, most likely derived from the movement of animals within the nesting area. The topography of the uppermost hypsilophodont nesting ground, as exposed by the 1982 vertical excavation of Egg Mountain, showed it to be a hummocky surface with an average of fifteen centimeters relief. No footprints or other recognizable biotic traces were observed. Polished sections of the top six to twelve centimeters show, however, traces of small, sediment-filled burrows, root casts, and suspended faunal remains (Fig. 4b). The hummocky surface is undoubtedly a fossil soil horizon (paleosol).

Surrounding Egg Mountain and Egg Island, at stratigraphic levels equivalent to the nesting horizons, are sediments of lacustrine origin (Lorenz and Gavin 1984). These lake sediments, in the immediate area of the nesting sites, are composed of

a sequence of silty to clean microcrystalline limestones (Lorenz and Gavin 1984). The clean limestones contain charophytes, plants which occur in shallow, quiet, alkaline waters (Peck 1957). About one kilometer south of Egg Mountain, where it is assumed that the lake depth increased, the limestones are replaced by gray to green siltstones. The presence of oscillation ripple marks indicates that the substrate was deposited above the wave base (Lorenz and Gavin 1984). Here freshwater clams and snails are found, as are extensive beds of stromatolites. To the north and east of Egg Mountain and Egg Island the lacustrine sediments gradually thin out and are replaced by sandstones, which were deposited by shallow, braided streams (Lorenz and Gavin 1984). Within the lake sediments the only fossil remains that have been found, other than the clams, snails, stromatolites, and charophytes, include a single crocodile tooth and a partial pterosaur wing described by Padian (1984). Abundant, isolated dinosaur remains have been found at the lakeshore braided-stream interface. Lorenz and Gavin (1984) state that the lake was most likely seasonal, evidenced by subaerially derived mud cracks. They also suggest that both Egg Mountain and Egg Island formed originally as small deltas or splay deposits and that they were eventually cut off from the main land body by rising lake levels. The limestone sediments of Egg Mountain and Egg Island were apparently derived from carbonate precipitation from a high water table afforded by the lake. Lorenz and Gavin assume that the original carbonates were derived from the paleozoic thrust sheets to the west.

Two types of eggs are found in the sediments of Egg Mountain (Horner 1984a). The most common are those attributed (identified on the basis of in situ embryonic skeletons) to an undescribed fabrosaurlike hypsilophodontid. Individual whole eggs (Fig. 5a) average about seventeen centimeters in length and seven centimeters in greatest latitudinal diameter. Most eggs of this kind are found to have been hatched, as they consist of the lower halves or thirds of the eggs (Fig. 5b) and contain numerous eggshell fragments derived from the upper portions of the eggs. To the unaided eye the eggs appear to have a smooth superficial texture, but when viewed under magnification (Fig. 5c), the surface possesses an abundance of parallel, low-relief grooves and ridges. These longitudinally oriented striations occur on the sides of the eggs and terminate before reaching the apex and nadir. Pores in the eggshell are found in the grooves. A more complete study of these and all other eggs from Egg Mountain and other localities in the vicinity of Willow Creek Anticline is being conducted by Karl Hirsch at the University of Colorado, Boulder.

The second type of egg from Egg Mountain is oval in shape (Fig. 6a) measuring approximately twelve centimeters in length and six centimeters in diameter. Except for the small ends of these eggs, the surface texture is bumpy (Fig. 6b). The individual bumps rise about 0.5 millimeters off the otherwise smooth surface and seldom run together. Pores are found exclusively in the smooth surfaces between bumps. Although the origin of these eggs is unknown, most are found unhatched and one has been found that contains an incompletely ossified embryonic skeleton. Unfortunately the skeleton is so small that its identity cannot be determined at present. As the specimen is too small and delicate

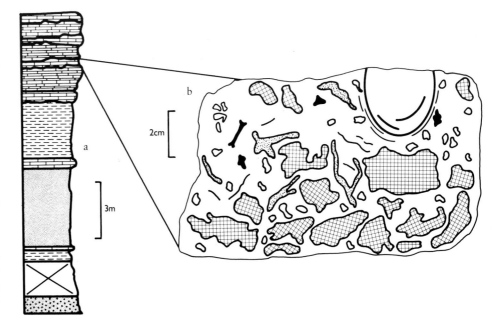

to be removed from the calcareous sediment, studies are being carried out using new X-ray and X-ray–computed tomography techniques.

Twelve hypsilophodont clutches, three of which were not exposed to surface weathering, were removed from the Egg Mountain site. The configuration of the eggs within these clutches is invariably a spiral pattern (Figs. 7 and 8). The lower eighth to one half of all hypsilophodont eggs are found in the upper part of the bioturbated calcareous siltstones. The remaining upper portions of these eggs are surrounded by calcareous mud-stone sediments. The elongate, ellipsoidal eggs are found upright or obliquely oriented (depending on their clutch position) and, except where an egg has clearly tipped over, do not touch one another. The space between the eggs averages about five millimeters at their upper ends and four centimeters at their lower ends. Of all the eggs found on Egg Mountain only a single clutch of twelve (Museum of the Rockies, MOR 299) was found unhatched and unscathed by processes of erosion. It is presently unknown whether these eggs contain the remains of embryos.

Figure 4. a. Stratigraphic section through Egg Mountain. Dots represent siltstone or sandstone, dashed lines represent shale, and brick design is same as in Figure 3. b. Drawing of polished section of calcareous siltstone caliche from lower nesting horizon. Black objects are bioclasts; small white objects are mud chips; irregular, dot-filled branchlike areas are root casts; blocky objects with screen patterns are disrupted original host rock; and the rounded object on the right represents the bottom end of an egg.

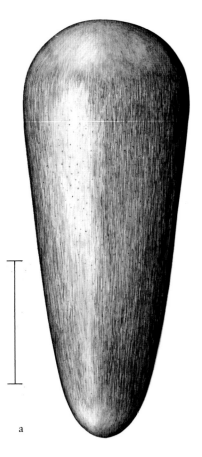

b

c

Figure 5. a. Drawing of whole hypsilophodont egg showing elongate ellipsoidal shape, longitudinal striations, and smooth ends. Scale is 5 centimeters. b. Two hatched hypsilophodont eggs (MOR 247) showing the portions most often found in situ. Note eggshell fragment within egg on right. Centimeter scale. c. Photo of the surface of hypsilophodont egg (MOR 247) showing grooves. Note very small pores. Millimeter scale.

Due in most part to weathering, the number of eggs found in a clutch varies from three to twenty-four (see Fig. 8). The clutches appear to have originally numbered either twelve or twenty-four eggs. Because most clutches consist of an even dozen eggs, it would seem that those with two dozen eggs might represent communal nests. This situation, particularly considering the spiral arrangement of the eggs, presents a number of behavioral problems. The first to consider is how the eggs were arranged, regardless of their original number. Granger (1936) suggested that the circular clutch arrangement of *Protoceratops* was a result of the female rotating her body as she deposited each egg in a circular, bowl-shaped nest. Granger also suggested, although doubted, that the female arranged the eggs with her front feet or beak. The eggs of *Protoceratops,* like those of many of the megapod birds, are found in layered circles. The eggs are oriented obliquely with their larger upper ends pointing toward the clutch center. Granger (1936) and Young (1965) suggest that the female deposited the lower circle, covered them with a layer of sand, then laid the second layer of eggs over the first. Young suggests that there may have been as many as four layers, although this has not been confirmed. The shape of the nest allowed the second tier of eggs to extend further from the center (for example see Young 1965: pl. II). The clutches of some megapod birds are arranged in much the same manner, and

it is presumed that this arrangement allows minimum obstruction for the hatchlings (Firth 1962) and optimal gas exchange (Mellon 1982).

The arrangement of eggs in the hypsilophodont nests is similar to those of *Protoceratops* and megapods in that the eggs are separated from one another and are generally oriented with their upper ends directed centrally. What is different, however, is the spiral arrangement and single layer of eggs. Although it is quite possible that the hypsilophodont female simply rotated her body during the egg-laying process, it seems improbable that the eggs would have been so perfectly placed. I find it difficult to believe that the female could deposit the eggs, each at a perfectly regulated depth, each evenly spaced, and each so very well oriented. I think it is more likely that the female deposited the eggs and then manipulated them with her front feet and beak. Clutches containing twenty-four eggs may have been the result of two deposits subsequently rearranged.

The arrangement of the bumpy textured eggs is very different from that of the hypsilophodonts in that the eggs seem to be lined up in rows (Fig. 9a). The eggs are invariably found lying on their sides with the egg axis parallel to the depositional surface. The eggs are found entirely within the bioturbated calcareous siltstone sediment (Fig. 9b). It is not known how many eggs constitute a clutch as some eggs are found isolated and others are found in groups of up to four. A clutch of these eggs is herein considered to consist of all eggs found in relatively close proximity to one another. In each instance where two eggs are found side by side (Fig. 9a) their vertical and anterior/posterior positions in the sediment are identical. Although the eggs, whether side by side or aligned end to end, do not touch one another, they are generally no more than two or three centimeters apart. If all of the eggs were end to end it would be possible that the animal simply laid one egg, moved a little, and laid another egg and so on, but the side by side arrangement is a puzzle. Again, it would seem that the female manipulated the eggs after deposition, not only to arrange the eggs but also to cover them with sediment.

As described in my article (1982a) concerning colonial nesting and site fidelity, many of the hypsilophodont clutches from Egg Mountain are found at distances from one another equivalent to the assumed length of an adult hypsilophodont (three meters). This is also true for the three nests found on Egg Island. There is no indication of clutch overlap or of clutches existing in the sediment zones between nesting horizons (see Fig. 3). These intermediate sediment zones do however yield occasional eggshell fragments and isolated skeletal elements. It is difficult to state with any certainty whether or not the nests found on a particular horizon represent concurrent nesting. The nests that occur on a particular horizon, however, do not vary in vertical perspective by more than the fifteen centimeters of relief found on the upper-nesting horizon. The evidence therefore strongly suggests that these dinosaurs nested in colonies and returned to the area successively for some period of time. This also appears to be the case for the animal that laid the bumpy eggs in linear rows, as its eggs are found on the same horizons as the hypsilophodont clutches. The occurrence of the bumpy unidentified eggs together with the hypsilophodont clutches suggests that some sort of symbiotic relationship existed between the two species (Horner 1984a).

Considering that the hatched hypsilophodont eggs are found as unbroken lower halves or thirds, it seems reasonable to assume that the hatchlings left their respective nests immediately after hatching. An abundance of articulated and isolated juvenile hypsilophodont skeletal remains found on or within the nest horizon sediments also suggests that the young did not leave the area until sometime much later in their lives. Based on comparative histologic studies of the hypsilophodont skeletal remains with those of other dinosaurs it appears that those hypsilophodonts that remained in the nesting areas were individuals of less than three quarters adult size (Peterson personal communication). This suggests that the mature adults may not have been attending to the young as I previously suggested (Horner 1984a). It does not, however, preclude the idea that the young remained in some sort of aggregation. As adult and subadult individuals (greater than one half adult size) are found in other sediments (adjacent to lake facies), it might have been that the young left their protective nesting areas after reaching a particular size (half grown).

The faunal assemblage found within the sediments of Egg Mountain appear to represent both autochthonous and allochthonous remains. The apparent autochthonous specimens are found exclusively on or within the bioturbated, gray, calcareous siltstone nest-horizon sediments. Included in these sediments are whole, partially articulated, or isolated skeletal remains of hypsilophodonts, varanid lizards, and mammals (multituberculates and marsupials). The hypsilophodont and other dinosaur remains of Egg Mountain are being studied by David Weishampel of Johns Hopkins University and me. The lizard material is currently being studied by Richard Estes of San Diego State University, and the mammal specimens are being studied by William Clemens of the University of California, Berkeley. Also found in these sediments are isolated teeth of the above mentioned animals plus those of the carnivorous dinosaurs *Troödon* and *Albertosaurus*. Commonly found on the nesting horizons, closely associated with the hypsilophodont nests (Fig. 10a), are casts of assumed insect or beetle pupal cases. Well-preserved specimens (Fig. 10b) show an external pattern that appears to consist of a tightly wound, fine threadlike structure similar to extant insect cocoons. Since these pupalike cases

Figure 6. a. "Bumpy" egg (MOR 301) in lateral view. b. Magnified surface of MOR 301. Millimeter scale.

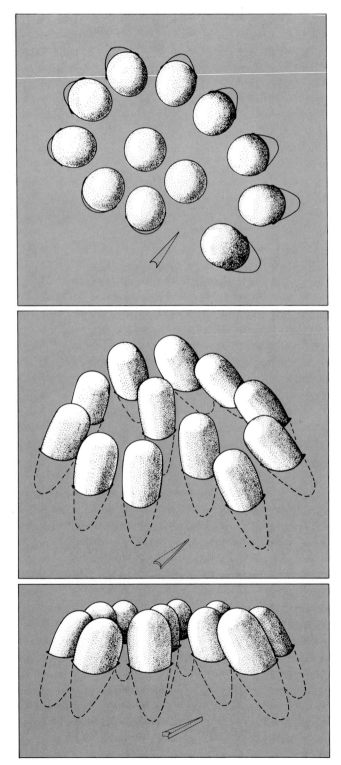

Figure 7. Drawing of hypsilophodont clutch (MOR 299) from apex, oblique, and lateral views showing spiral configuration of clutch and relative position of eggs. Lower shaded area represents portion of eggs within the limy siltstone. Upper areas encased in mudstone matrix.

are commonly found associated with all nests and skeletons it is assumed that the insects or beetles were scavenging carcasses and egg fluids. Terrestrial gastropods of the family *Polygyraeidae* are also commonly found in the nest-horizon sediments.

It appears from the nesting horizon faunal list that all of the animals, both vertebrate and invertebrate, had an ecologic relationship, most likely relating to the dinosaur eggs and young. Varanid lizards, for example, are well-documented predators of megapod (Lincoln 1974) and crocodilian (Magnusson 1982) egg clutches. Mammals such as raccoons have also been observed digging up nests (Kushland and Kushland 1980), so it is possible that the mammal inhabitants of Egg Mountain were also occasional egg stealers. The small carnivorous dinosaur *Troödon* may also have eaten eggs, although its likely prey would have been the hatched young. The albertosaurs could have preyed on any of the inhabitants. The diet of the hypsilophodonts is questionable, due mainly to the fact that these animals possessed heterodont, fabrosaurlike teeth. As pointed out by Thulborn (1971), the maxillary teeth appear to have been primarily used for grinding up plant material, whereas the pointed and slightly recurved premaxillary teeth look as if they may have been used for ripping flesh. It may be that these hypsilophodonts were omnivorous or possibly insectivorous. Or, as suggested by Thulborn, the premaxillary teeth may have been adapted for use on a particular kind of plant endemic to a semiarid environment.

Within the calcareous mud stones between nesting horizons rare fragmentary remains of hadrosaurs and tyrannosaurs have been collected, as has an articulated teiid lizard. Most of the hadrosaur and carnosaur remains include worn, shed teeth. Eggshell fragments of at least three species (hypsilophodont, unidentified bumpy, and hadrosaur) have also been found as isolated bioclasts. The amount and kinds of faunal remains found in these sediments are very similar to those found in other sediments of the Willow Creek Anticline where nests are absent. It is possible, therefore, that the sediments between nesting horizons originated, as suggested by Lorenz and Gavin (1984), as

a

b

Figure 8. Hypsilophodont clutches of 10 (a, PU 22591) and 24 (b, MOR 394) eggs. Eggs are upside-down; centimeter scale.

splay or deltaic deposits during times when the lake had subsided and that the faunal remains are allochthonous.

The only vertebrate remains found on Egg Island were nineteen in situ embryonic hypsilophodont skeletons. As mentioned earlier however, the site was neither screened nor excavated. A few terrestrial gastropods and pupal cases were found. Within the eggs containing the embryos are numerous oblong fecal pellets of unknown origin. These pellets average 1.5 millimeters in length and 0.75 millimeters in latitudinal diameter. The pellets are very similar to those present in a fossil crane egg (identified by Karl Hirsch, University of Colorado) from the Eocene Willwood Formation of Wyoming (Princeton University, PU 18847). It is not known what killed the near fully developed hypsilophodont embryos, but it is clear that the soft tissues were eaten by small invertebrates (possibly maggots). There is no indication that any of the eggs were crushed, broken, or scavenged by larger animals.

Of the identifiable faunal remains only the hypsilophodonts are assumed to have been endemic to the upper coastal plain environment. Although incompletely studied, morphologic characteristics suggest that these small ornithopods were generically distinct from all other described hypsilophodonts except for the specimen described by Gilmore (1924) and named *"Laosaurus" minimus.* This specimen was also derived from upper coastal plain sediments (Belly River Formation, as noted by Russell 1949) located in Alberta, Canada.

The lake fauna consisted of bivalves, gastropods, and algae. The single isolated crocodile tooth was most likely transported in from some other area as there was little if anything for these archosaurs to have fed on. The absence of fish remains in the lake deposits is probably due to the combination of the lake having been alkaline and intermittent. The adjacent stream deposits lack aquatic vertebrate fauna as well.

Geologic data indicate that Egg Island was, as its name suggests, an island located near the northern shore of a shallow, alkaline lake. Egg Mountain may also have been an island, although equivalent age strata are missing to the east of the site. It was, however, also located near the shore line of the lake, which Gavin (personal communication) believes may have had a total surface area of about ten to fifteen square kilometers. Both islands appear to have been relatively small, with surface areas most likely not exceeding five thousand square meters.

The lake, and probably many more like it, existed on the upper coastal plain within forty kilometers of the mountains produced by Sevier thrusting and some local volcanoes. Between 100

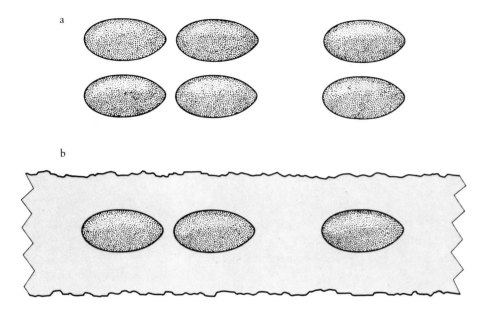

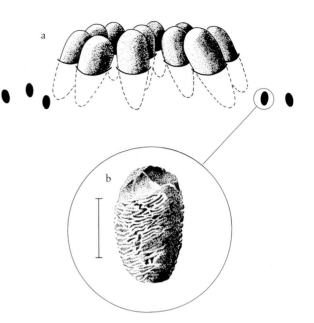

Figure 9. Clutch of six "bumpy" eggs as seen from above (a) and laterally (b). Shaded area represent limy siltstone matrix.

Figure 10. Drawing showing relative position of assumed insect or beetle pupa cases with egg clutch (a), and drawing of single pupa case showing external surface pattern (b). Scale is 1 cm.

to 250 kilometers to the east existed the western shore of the Western Interior Cretaceous Seaway. The lake and braided-stream deposits were one of two alternating sedimentary sequences that Gavin (personal communication) believes reflect local changes in the slope gradient of the coastal plain. Above and beneath the lake facies are sediments of anastomosing stream channels and extensively oxidized flood-plain deposits, which yield the remains of hadrosaur nests. The hadrosaur nest sites are exclusive to banks of anastomosing rivers. It appears, therefore, that the dinosaurs had preferred nesting habitats.

Relief on the coastal plain appears to have been minimal, confined primarily to the relief of individual interfluves.

Vegetation, as indicated by root casts in caliches, occasional bituminous clasts in shale deposits, rare fossilized (completely replaced) wood, and pollen, suggests that the lake and streams were fringed by trees and the islands had a cover of small plants. Unfortunately, however, as explained by Retallack (1984) the highly calcareous sediments (caliches) found in this area are of the type in which plant material is most often not preserved. Although pollen has been extracted from sediments in the area, none of the pollen species can be correlated with specific plant species.

Gavin (personal communication) interprets the well-developed caliches found on Egg Mountain and Egg Island as having originated in semiarid environments consisting of long dry spells interrupted by seasonal rainfall of one hundred to five hundred millimeters annually. Transport of the original carbonates, in the form of dust, from the Cordilleran high is suggested to have been accomplished primarily by wind rather than fluvial means. Gavin believes the westerly winds, which originated off the proto-Pacific, were prevalent during most of the fall, winter, and spring months. He further suggests that the moisture from the proto-Pacific was dropped on the west side of the mountains, leaving a rain shadow over the upland nesting region. During summer months, rains derived from convective storms originated over the Western Interior Cretaceous Seaway and moved westward. Interpreting studies by Semeniuk and Meager (1981), Gavin suggests that the rainy period was relatively short, the temperatures were high, the humidity was low, and winds were common. Based on interpretive studies of mid-Cretaceous climate by Lloyd (1982) the interior seaway surface temperatures in the region that would have been adjacent to the nesting area apparently varied from about sixteen degrees Celsius in January to twenty-four degrees C in July.

The object of this paper has been to present the information relevant to the understanding of the ecology and general behavior of animals that inhabited a dinosaur-nesting site. Obviously the information can be interpreted many different ways and most likely will be as further information comes in from other sites. The following scenario, written as if it were a generalized naturalistic study in recent times and dealing with extant animals, expresses my feeling of what these data suggest for a period of time some eighty million years before present.

Viewed from the air (Fig. 11), one of several small islands slightly breaks the surface near the northern shore of a shallow lake. Large pterosaurs glide in a circling pattern on rising thermals, waiting for a chance to prey on unsuspecting residents. A combination of dense algae and considerable particulate matter in the alkaline waters gives the lake a milky green color. It is late spring, and winds blowing out of the east bring in hot weather and occasional thunderstorms borne over the interior seaway. The lake level apparently rises during this season, affording the residents of the islands an added sense of protection from many predators. On each of the small islands, there exist numerous one-meter-diameter nest depressions in close proximity to one another. Small plants grow near the island's shore, and larger plants and trees exist along the lake shore.

Within the lake the molluscan fauna and algal flora are confined to areas close to the mouths of streams where fresh waters provide adequate living conditions. Fishes and amphibians are either very rare or nonexistent as they are not observed.

At ground level numerous island inhabitants are observed. The largest are bipedal, three-meter-long hypsilophodont dinosaurs, which are actively tending nests of eggs, some of which appear to be hatching. Adult hypsilophodonts remove vegetation and sediment that cover the top portions of the ellipsoidal eggs. Each of the eggs appears to have been very carefully arranged so as not to touch another during incubation. The clutches of twelve or twenty-four eggs are each arranged in spiral patterns. Where vegetation has been removed the young are hatching by popping off the tops of the eggs and exiting the nests. The emerging hatchlings

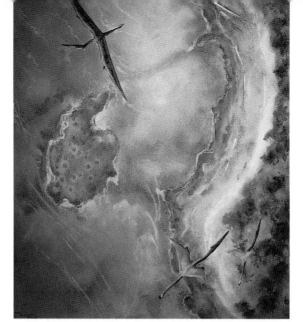

Figure 11. Restoration of the Egg Mountain nesting site as seen from above. Pastel by Doug Henderson. See also page x.

Figure 12. Pencil restoration by Doug Henderson of varanid lizards invading hypsilophodont nest.

Figure 13. Aggregate group of adult and half grown hypsilophodonts moving away from nesting ground. Pastel by Doug Henderson. See also page xi.

Figure 14. Early pastel restoration by Doug Henderson of the Egg Mountain nesting area.

are relatively large. The elongate, ellipsoidal eggs allow a relatively small adult the capability of having a large hatchling. Although remaining together on their island nesting site, the young appear to be quite capable of precocial activity. Some of the nests appear to be intact but unattended, whereas others appear to have been destroyed by scavengers. A pair of varanid lizards are seen raiding one of the unattended nests (Fig. 12). Skeletal remains of small mammals are occasionally found near the nests, but it is unclear whether they were predators, prey, or innocent bystanders. Beetles and other insects take advantage of the hatching, feeding on fluids from the eggs and dead embryos.

Diet of the hypsilophodonts seems to be varied and probably age dependent. The hatchlings begin by feeding on adult feces, from which they apparently derive the fermentative microbes necessary for a herbivorous diet (see Rogers 1985). It appears that the young then begin feeding on plants and small insects. Larger individuals and adults appear to be omnivorous.

The young hypsilophodonts remain in the nesting area, protected by a few adults, while other adults wade or swim to feed along the lake shore.

By the end of summer, as the lake recedes and the island is connected to the main land mass, the adults and young move out into other areas (Fig. 13). By this time the young are large and swift enough to escape most predators.

In 1982 I wrote a short article about the discoveries at Willow Creek Anticline (Horner 1982b) in which artist Doug Henderson attempted to reconstruct particular habitats including Egg Mountain. The information collected over the previous three summers was used for a restoration (Fig. 14). At that time there were several aspects about the nesting site that were unknown, and as is nearly always the case when information is lacking, the interpretation and restoration were somewhat incorrect. The island was depicted as being rather large and partly covered with large trees. And the hypsilophodonts were restored as much too lean and described as carnivores. By collecting specimens and data during the following three seasons we gained a much clearer idea of life on Egg Mountain. Nevertheless, we are still lacking important geologic and morphologic information, which will allow future restorations to be closer to the truth.

would have had such s
gans, etc. But this was
vided with the means t
sion must have used its
did not keep them fold
position would have b
again like birds; so, lik
erect and recurved bac
would not lose all eq
translation).

Cuvier's pronouncen
and his inferences tha
ture, were not univer
ers, especially in Ga
yielding more specin
mal. Some thought
amphibious), others
it was considered a
reptiles and birds, b
bats. The question o
both was still active
tirely settled even a
1975; Padian 1979
seemed to have beer
was of a lizardlike,
powers of flapping f
poor internal struct
ankles.

Later studies
phology, and evoluti
tation of pterosaurs
winged gliders seen
accounts, newer res
more likely warm-b
tively narrow and c
they were superb act
on their hind limbs l
are their closest rel
1978; Padian 1983
been put forth by ea
other, but for the m
supported by anatc
popular and scient
the traditional bat-
gliding reptiles, wit
membranes extend

Acknowledgments

Special thanks are extended to artists D. Hender-son, who provided the reconstructions, and K. El-lingsen (Figs. 3, 4, 7–10) and P. Longobardi (Fig. 5a) for their technical drawings. Many thanks to R. T. Bakker and three other reviewers. Photo-graphs were taken by S. Jackson. The project was funded by National Science Foundation Grant EAR 8007817 and 8305173 and a grant from MONTS/EPSCOR.

Works Cited

Firth, H. J. 1962. *The Mallee fowl.* Sydney: Angus & Robertson.

Gilmore, C. W. 1924. A new species of *Laosaurus,* an ornithischian dinosaur from the Cretaceous of Alberta. *Transactions of the Royal Society of Canada,* sec. IV, 3d ser. 18: 3–6.

Granger, W. 1936. The story of dinosaur eggs. *Natural History* 38, no. 1: 21–25.

Horner, J. R. 1982a. Evidence of colonial nesting and "site fidelity" among ornithischian dinosaurs. *Nature* 297: 675–76.

———. 1982b. Coming home to roost. *Montana Outdoors* 13, no. 4: 2–5.

———. 1984a. The nesting behavior of dinosaurs. *Scientific American* 250, no. 4: 130–37.

———. 1984b. Three ecologically distinct vertebrate faunal communities from the Late Cretaceous Two Medicine Formation of Montana, with discussion of the evolutionary pressures induced by interior seaway fluctuations. In *Montana Geological Society 1984 Field Conference, Northwestern Montana,* 299–303.

Horner, J. R., and R. Makela. 1979. Nest of juveniles provides evidence of family structure among dinosaurs. *Nature* 282: 296–98.

Kushland, J. K., and M. S. Kushland. 1980. Function of nest attendance in the American alligator. *Herpetologica* 36, no. 1: 27–32.

Lincoln, G. A. 1974. Predation of incubator birds (*Megapodius frecinet*) by Komodo dragons (*Varanus komodoensis*). *Journal of Zoology* (London) 174: 419–28.

Lloyd, C. R. 1982. The mid-Cretaceous earth: Paleogeography; ocean circulation and temperature; atmospheric circulation. *Journal of Geology* 90: 393–413.

Lorenz, J. C. 1981. Sedimentary and tectonic history of the Two Medicine Formation, Late Cretaceous (Campanian), northwestern Montana. Ph.D. diss., Princeton University.

Lorenz, J. C., and W. Gavin. 1984. Geology of the Two Medicine Formation and the sedimentology of a dinosaur nesting ground. In *Montana Geological Society 1984 Field Conference, Northwestern Montana,* 175–86.

Magnusson, W. E. 1982. Mortality of eggs of the crocodile *Crocodylus porosus* in northern Australia. *Journal of Herpetology* 16, no. 2: 121–30.

Mellon, R. M. 1982. Behavioral implications of dinosaur nesting patterns. Senior thesis, Department of Geology, Princeton University.

Padian, K. 1984. A large pterodactyloid pterosaur from the Two Medicine Formation (Campanian) of Montana. *Journal of Vertebrate Paleontology* 4, no. 4: 516–24.

Peck, R. E. 1957. North American Mesozoic Charophyta. *United States Geological Society Professional Paper,* 294: 1–44.

Retallack, G. 1984. Completeness of the rock and fossil record: Some estimates using fossil soils. *Paleobiology* 10, no. 1: 59–78.

Rogers, K. L. 1985. Possible physiological and behavioral adaptations of herbivorous dinosaurs. *Journal of Vertebrate Paleontology* 5, no. 4: 371–72.

Russell, L. S. 1949. The relationships of the Alberta Cretaceous dinosaur "*Laosaurus*" *minimus* Gilmore. *Journal of Paleontology* 23, no. 5: 518–20.

Semeniuk, V., and T. D. Meager. 1981. Calcrete in Quaternary coastal dunes in southwestern Australia: A capillary-rise phenomenon associated with plants. *Journal of Sedimentary Petrology* 51, no. 1: 47–68.

Thulborn, R. A. 1971. Tooth wear and jaw action in the Triassic ornithischian dinosaur *Frabrosaurus. Journal of Zoology* (London) 164: 165–79.

Young, C. C. 1965. Fossil eggs from Nanhsiung, Kwangtung and Kanchou, Kiangsi. *Vertebrata PalAsiatica* 9, no. 2: 141–70.

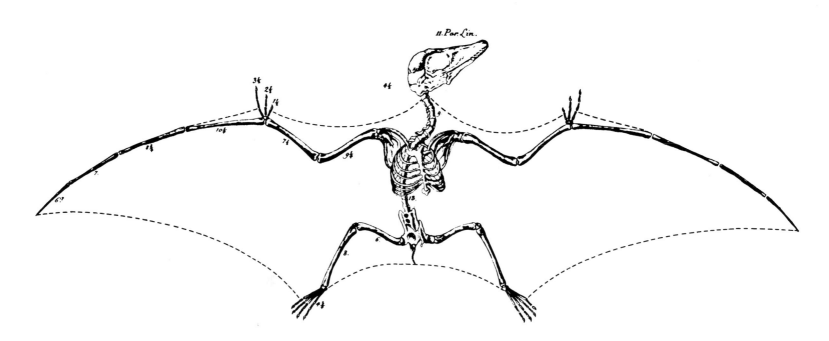

11.Par.Lin.

Figure 2. Reconstruction of *Pterodactylus* ("*Ornithocephalus*") *brevirostris,* by Th. von Soemmerring (1817).

EARLY RESTORATIONS OF PTEROSAURS

The conflicting interpretations of pterosaurs held by the naturalists of the early nineteenth century produced a flurry of strange restorations. Although many were fanciful, others were based on careful, if often unverifiable, inferences of soft part structures. Their history provides insight into the establishment of the "bat-winged" image of pterosaurs through a particular chain of reconstruction founded on an early error in identification.

Abel (1925) chronicled much of the history of pterosaurian reconstruction and pointed out that depictions of pterosaurs in the popular literature of the nineteenth century far outnumbered those in scientific publications. Meyer, for instance, does not seem to have attempted any reconstructions, although he published nearly thirty works on pterosaurs. The lack of interest among paleontologists in presenting lifelike conceptions of pterosaurs evidently did not satisfy the public, and many uninformed and inaccurate portraits were produced.

The earliest known pterosaurian restoration—a batlike *Pterodactylus* "revêtu de son poil"—was sent to Cuvier around the turn of the nineteenth century by Professor Herrmann of Strasbourg, but has since been lost. Abel believed that the oldest surviving restoration would therefore be that of Johann Wagler (1830), who restored *Pterodactylus* as a swimming animal (Fig. 1). But earlier still is the skeletal reconstruction of *Ornitho-*

cephalus brevirostris by Soemmerring (1817; now considered a juvenile *Pterodactylus*), with the outline of the wings represented by a dotted line (Fig. 2). In this drawing the membrane extends from the tip of the wings posteriorly to the ankles and continues to connect the hind limbs and the short tail. In front of the main wing a propatagial surface extends between the three small fingers of the manus and the anterior cervical vertebrae. This particular drawing is important for two reasons: first, because, although it did not influence later German workers, it played a key part in the subsequent Anglo-American literature; and second, because Soemmerring believed that the animal he described was not a reptile but a bat.

Soemmerring's drawing was adapted by Buckland for the widely read *Bridgewater treatise* of 1836 (note no. 42 in Fig. 3). This was quite possibly the earliest reconstruction of a pterosaur to appear in England, although Buckland, like most workers by that time, did not agree that pterosaurs were bats; in fact, he referred to them in his text as bipeds. But in the same volume Buckland included his own portrayal of pterosaurs in their life habit (Fig. 4); the broad wings, connected to the ankles and spanning the interfemoral area, seem to have been directly influenced by Soemmerring's figure.

The pterosaur represented in this picture is "*Pterodactylus*" *macronyx,* from the Early Jurassic of Lyme Regis, of which Buckland had earlier described some postcranial remains. Buckland had mistaken the caudal (tail) vertebrae for cervical (neck) vertebrae, which explains the long neck and short tail of his figure. Pterodactyloid pterosaurs, such as Collini's (1784) original, had short tails; the long tails that distinguish the more primitive rhamphorhynchoids were not recognized as diagnostic until 1846. When the skull of Buckland's Lyme Regis pterosaur was finally found, it proved to be so different from the German forms that Owen (1858) rechristened his animal *Dimorphodon*, on the basis of the small lancet-shaped teeth found posterior to the large laniaries of the lower jaw. Long before, Buckland had ascribed an isolated lower jaw to the as yet undiscovered skull of this pterosaur; Owen had believed that the jaw belonged to a fish.

At this point I wish to suggest that the popular reconstruction of pterosaurs assumed an important role in establishing the acceptance of the bat-winged image, in spite of the lack of evidence then or now for it. Reconstructions in the German

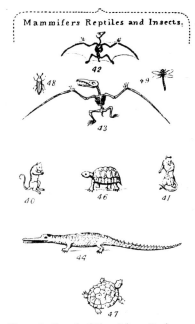

Figure 3. Detail of Plate I from Buckland's (1836) volumes on Geology and Mineralogy of the *Bridgewater treatise*, showing his adaptation (No. 42) of Soemmerring's reconstruction of *Ornithocephalus*.

scientific literature are conspicuously absent before the 1880s. There is no evidence in the scientific literature of that time for narrow wings; no other pterosaurian remains were described in England until Owen reworked *Dimorphodon* in 1870, with the exception of fragmentary bones from the Gault and the Cambridge Greensand, described by both Owen and Seeley before 1870. Buckland's drawings, based as they were on complete and well-known German specimens, were evidently regarded as authoritative, for there was no reason to suspect that an alternate wing configuration was plausible. This image persisted in other semipopular accounts, such as the English translation of *La Terre avant le déluge* by L. Figuier (1866), *Book of the great sea-dragons* by T. Hawkins (1840), or even *Manual of geology* by J. Phillips (1855), (Fig. 5). As it was gradually understood that pterosaurs were reptiles, the resemblances to birds, stressed so much by Meyer, faded and were replaced by a more reptilian image. The evidence for this subtle psychological ensconcement is admittedly negative: in the absence of reconstructions to the contrary, and in the absence of contemporary evidence either way for the configuration of the pterosaur wing, I submit only that the earliest suggestion became the established one, as it so frequently has in historical interpretations of fossil animals. Buckland used Soemmerring's reconstruction, which was based on a misidentification, and other reconstructions published in England (by Figuier, Hawkins, and Phillips) can be easily derived from this inaccuracy. In the absence of English specimens to the contrary, and in the further absence of German narrow-winged reconstructions before 1882, it is reasonable to conclude that this chain of events established the bat-winged image by default.

THE SCIENTIFIC TRANSMISSION OF THE "BAT-WINGED" PTEROSAUR

In his redescription of *Dimorphodon* in 1870 Owen reproduced the bat-winged model (Fig. 6) without explaining his reasons for extending the wing to the foot, except to add that the two phalanges of the unusual fifth toe "have proportions and forms which clearly show their adaptive rela-

Figure 5. Nineteenth-century restorations of pterosaurs from (a) Newman 1843, (b) Hawkins 1840, (c) Phillips 1855, and (d and e) Figuier 1866. Note that the wings are connected to the legs in each restoration, however fanciful.

tions as aids in sustaining the interfemoral or caudofemoral parachute." The absence of justification for this statement is evidence of both the primacy of Owen's authority in the field and the establishment of the bat-winged image in the English scientific literature by that time. If the configuration of the pterosaur wing had been an issue, Owen would not have missed the opportunity to fit whichever reconstruction he regarded as correct into his world view of typology, anti-Darwinism, and "purely adaptive" features masking true taxonomic affinities (Desmond 1979, 1982; Padian 1980, 1985). I believe that his failure to do so speaks eloquently for the prevalence of the bat-winged image of pterosaurs at that time. The only contemporary statement that can even be considered to differ is in *Ornithosauria*, by Seeley (1870a), in which Seeley allowed that the organization of these animals probably varied according to the differing habits of the various forms. Although Seeley said that the wing was "comparable to that of a Bat in texture, but more comparable to a Bird in its extent," he

immediately afterward produced the puzzling statement that "the groups with long hind-legs probably had the membrane limited to the bones of the arm, while in the species with small hind-legs it may have attained even as great a development as in Bats, though there is no reason for suspecting that it extended to the tail" (Seeley 1870a: 104). Pterosaurs are not readily divided into long- and short-legged forms; inasmuch as Seeley produced no restoration of the material he described, it is difficult to envision exactly what he had in mind. It is also difficult to see how his statement could have countered the image of *Dimorphodon* evoked by Owen's restoration. Seeley's vagueness on this point extended to his restorations in *Dragons of the air* (1901) where, for instance, he portrayed *Dimorphodon* (a long-legged form?) as both a biped and a quadruped and extended the wings to the feet.

The predominance of Owen's reconstruction in the English literature clearly extended to America. In 1882 Yale's O. C. Marsh described a

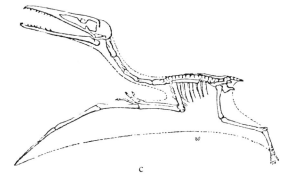

c

e

Rhamphorhynchus specimen from the Sölnhofen limestones that he had bought for the Yale College Museum through a friend in Germany. Marsh included a restoration (Fig. 7) that, far from being a detailed morphological summary of the animal at hand, was merely a copy of Owen's *Dimorphodon* (Fig. 6) with the head altered to correspond to that of *Rhamphorhynchus* and with the addition of the characteristic leaf-shaped tail vane he used to name the new species *phyllurus*. Ironically Marsh also provided a lithograph of the specimen, which was the first ever found with impressions of the wings preserved; the lithograph differs from his restoration in showing that the hind limbs were free of the wing (Fig. 8). This is in fact the case with the specimen, as K. A. von Zittel (1882), writing at Munich in the same year as Marsh, pointed out in describing other newly found German specimens with traces of wings preserved (Wellnhofer 1978; Padian 1979, 1983b). One especially complete specimen of an isolated wing in the Bayerische Staatssammlung provided Zittel with incontrovertible evidence.

d

The narrow width of this fully preserved wing membrane, which is sharply defined on all sides, is striking when compared to the considerable length of the wing. . . . The flight organ of the rhamphorhynchids was somewhat comparable to the wing of a swallow or gull and was considerably more slender than the restoration figured by Marsh (Zittel 1882; my translation).

However, Zittel's discovery and his accompanying restoration (Fig. 9) had little effect on the English and American literature. The bat-winged model was separately taken up by S. W. Williston and G. F. Eaton, both of whom worked on the American Cretaceous pterodactyloids in the Yale Peabody Museum during and after Marsh's tenure there. As no wings have ever been found preserved with these American forms, there would have been no reason to accept or doubt Marsh's reconstruction. Williston (1911) even went so far as to note:

That the membrane extended to the tarsus on the peroneal side of the legs I think now hardly admits of doubt; the animals would hardly have been "flugfähig" were the

Figure 6. Owen's (1870) restoration of *Dimorphodon*. Compare to Figures 13 and 14.

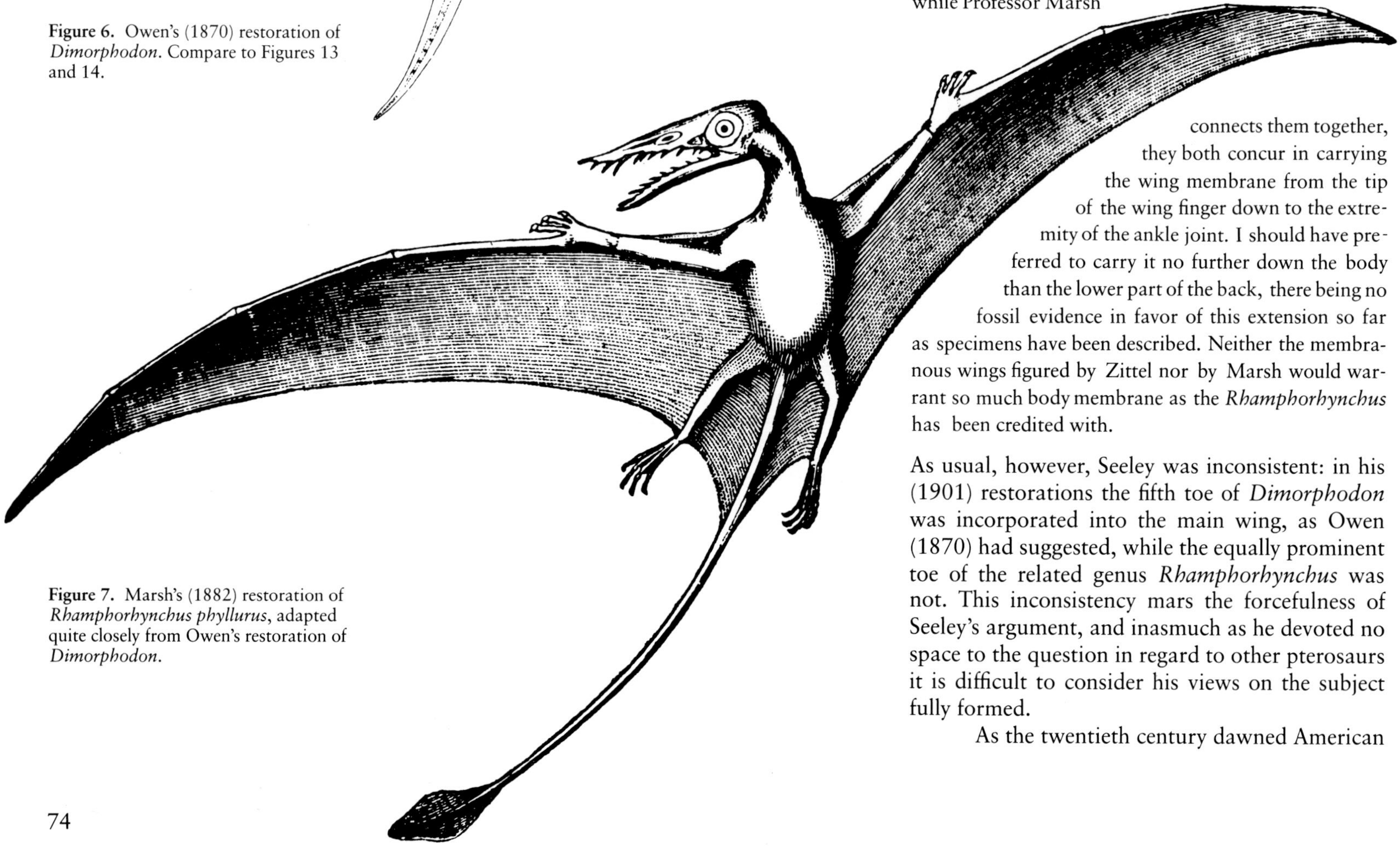

Figure 7. Marsh's (1882) restoration of *Rhamphorhynchus phyllurus*, adapted quite closely from Owen's restoration of *Dimorphodon*.

legs wholly free, since the wing membrane would have been too narrow to serve as a parachute, and since the legs with their attached membrane must have functioned much like the tail feathers of modern birds in the control of flight.

He further added that without the uropatagium, or membrane between the legs, the hind limbs would have had to exert constant muscular force against the pull of wings—a job for which, he asserted, they were much too frail. (Restorations of *Pteranodon* by Williston [1911] and Eaton [1910] are given in Figs. 10–11.)

Once again Seeley (1901: 165) provided the lone dissenting voice:

I cannot quite concur with either Professor Zittel or Professor Marsh in the expansion which they give to the wing membrane in their restorations; for although Professor Zittel represents the tail as free from the hind legs, while Professor Marsh connects them together, they both concur in carrying the wing membrane from the tip of the wing finger down to the extremity of the ankle joint. I should have preferred to carry it no further down the body than the lower part of the back, there being no fossil evidence in favor of this extension so far as specimens have been described. Neither the membranous wings figured by Zittel nor by Marsh would warrant so much body membrane as the *Rhamphorhynchus* has been credited with.

As usual, however, Seeley was inconsistent: in his (1901) restorations the fifth toe of *Dimorphodon* was incorporated into the main wing, as Owen (1870) had suggested, while the equally prominent toe of the related genus *Rhamphorhynchus* was not. This inconsistency mars the forcefulness of Seeley's argument, and inasmuch as he devoted no space to the question in regard to other pterosaurs it is difficult to consider his views on the subject fully formed.

As the twentieth century dawned American

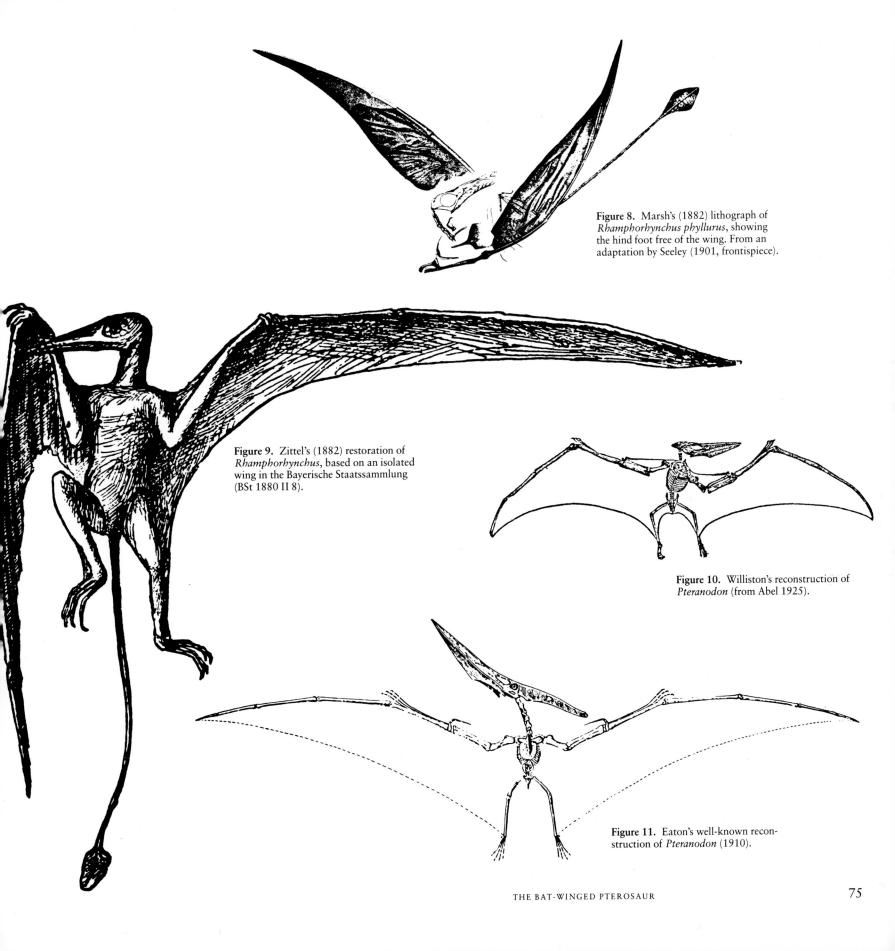

Figure 8. Marsh's (1882) lithograph of *Rhamphorhynchus phyllurus*, showing the hind foot free of the wing. From an adaptation by Seeley (1901, frontispiece).

Figure 9. Zittel's (1882) restoration of *Rhamphorhynchus*, based on an isolated wing in the Bayerische Staatssammlung (BSt 1880 II 8).

Figure 10. Williston's reconstruction of *Pteranodon* (from Abel 1925).

Figure 11. Eaton's well-known reconstruction of *Pteranodon* (1910).

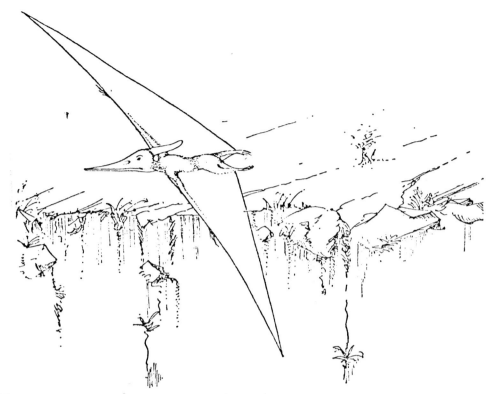

Figure 12. Restoration of *Pteranodon* gliding off a cliff (after Bramwell and Whitfield 1974: fig. 49; courtesy The Royal Society, London).

and British aeronautical engineers turned to paleontological knowledge of large pterosaurs to provide them with models from which to design their earliest aircraft. The only choice was the bat-winged version, shown for example in the excellent study by Hankin and Watson (1914). Author of *Animal flight* (1913), Hankin was a biological chemist who spent several years studying the soaring flight of birds on the Agra Plain of India. He appears to have independently discovered thermals and to have recognized them as a major source of soaring energy. Watson, the eminent British paleontologist, collaborated with Hankin on the study of *Pteranodon* and also made a series of notes on flight in pterosaurs published posthumously (1974). The detailed demonstration of the mechanical control of the wings of *Pteranodon* by Hankin and Watson was so impressive that it was modernized almost wholesale by Bramwell and Whitfield (1974) in their aerodynamic study. (Their reconstruction is given in Fig. 12.) Stein (1975) and others also adopted the broad-winged model for aerodynamic studies of *Pteranodon*, although Stein frankly admitted the possibility that the wings did not extend to the legs (see also von Kripp 1943; von

Holst 1957; Heptonstall 1971; Pennycuick 1972; Sneyd, Bundock, and Reid 1982; and a host of other popular and semipopular efforts).

Thus, a series of connections can be made from the initial misclassification of a juvenile *Pterodactylus* as an aberrant bat to the modern aerodynamic studies of 160 years later. It is perhaps ironic that, as the reptilian classification of pterosaurs gained success, so did the chiropteran view of their wings. But, as Cuvier (1812) noted, the idea of a flying reptile is truly self-contradictory, and we would not know what to expect such an animal to be like in life. The absence of feathers and the apparent support of the wing by a single finger, coupled with the suggestion (Padian 1979) that pterosaurs could have been considered inferior fliers simply because they were extinct, makes it unsurprising that the paleontological evidence to the contrary did not succeed in overthrowing the baseless reconstruction perpetuated from Soemmerring's early drawing. Nor is it surprising that the many birdlike aspects of the skeleton noted by Cuvier, Seeley, and others, which clearly indicate advanced flight metabolism, could have been ignored in favor of inferences drawn from certain primitive reptilian skeletal features only remotely connected to the metabolism of flight (see Desmond 1975; Padian 1979, 1983b).

THE ROLES OF PICTORIALIZATION AND CLASSIFICATION

Two important themes permeate the history of thought about pterosaurs. The first is the role of pictorialization in scientific understanding (Gombrich 1961; Rudwick 1976a, b). A picture is not only worth a thousand words; however inaccurate, it may be worth a wealth of well-documented evidence to the contrary. An early example is the long disregard in England, Germany, and the United States of Cuvier's analysis of the life habits and systematic placement of the "ptero-dactyle," and the preference for Soemmerring's tangible, but incorrect, reconstruction of it as a bat. (Unfortunately it is difficult to ascertain the contribution to the tradition made by the inaccessibility of foreign literature or the inability of many workers to read it, to say nothing of simple chauvinism, which may partly explain the disregard for Cuvier's opinion outside France.) Soemmerring had reassembled the skeleton in a stylized dissectional position, complete with the outline of the membrane drawn in; Cuvier had only faithfully reproduced (with corrections) the specimen as it was discovered in the "road-kill" position typical of most fossil skeletons. The subsequent chain of derivations, from Soemmerring to Buckland, Owen, Marsh, Eaton, Williston, Bramwell and Whitfield, Stein, and others, proceeded with almost no acknowledgment of evidence to the contrary (such as Zittel's) and was not supported by independent evidence. Popular reconstructions were inextricable in Gestalt from scientific ones, if less accurate in anatomical detail (Abel 1925; Desmond 1975). Even Zittel, who recognized the narrowness of the wing, provided a restoration in which the trailing edge, after arcing gull-like toward the waist of *Rhamphorhynchus*, suddenly dips to attach to the ankle.

The inference, explicit or implicit, was that the pterosaur wing lacked internal support and therefore had to be braced by the hind limb. The question of whether pterosaurs actively flew or merely glided was chronically muddled, but the prevalent belief was that that the wing membrane, which lacked the bat's reinforcing fingers, was made of leathery skin like the bat's wing and was even more like the unstructured airfoil of gliding squirrels. This accorded with the general notion of pterosaurs as lizardlike reptiles incapable of true flight and appeared to lend support to arguments made by Owen (1842) and others that the air was denser during the Mesozoic era, when pterosaurs could fly and gigantic sauropod dinosaurs could walk upright on land.

Gombrich (1961) has used the fantastic representations of lions, locusts, whales, and rhinos by artists from the thirteenth to the eighteenth centuries to illustrate the same point I make here about fossil animals. The starting point for the unfamil-

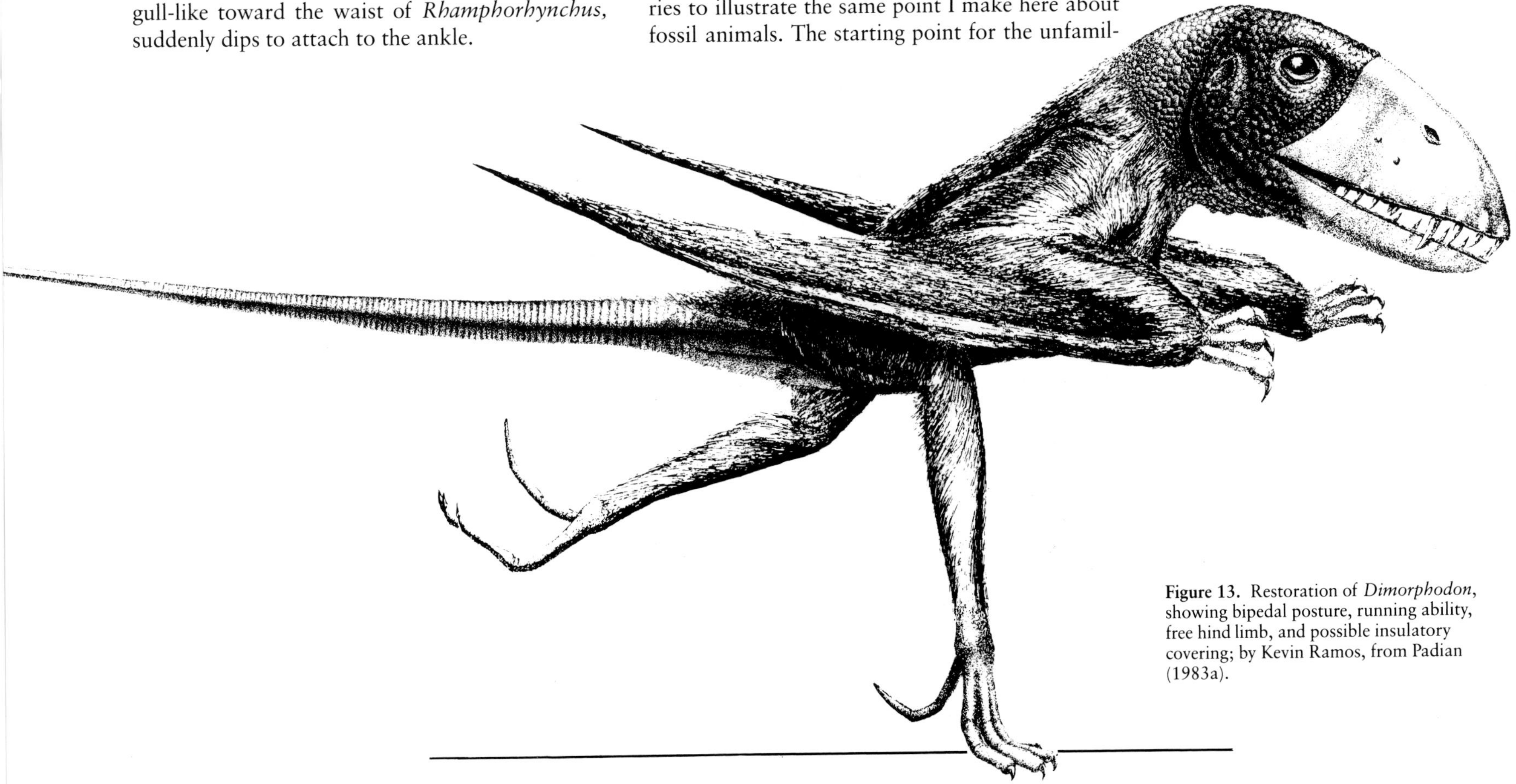

Figure 13. Restoration of *Dimorphodon*, showing bipedal posture, running ability, free hind limb, and possible insulatory covering; by Kevin Ramos, from Padian (1983a).

hind limb drawn out sideways to anchor the trailing edge of the airfoil as in bats. The consequences of this presumption, which invested nearly 160 years of pictorial reconstructions, were compounded by typological classification of pterosaurs as reptiles, which effectively prevented them from being anything other than "lizardlike" in physiology and suggested inferiority to the warm-blooded birds and bats. The image persisted despite evidence and arguments to the contrary, including Zittel's description of well-preserved impressions of narrow pterosaur wings as early as 1882 and Seeley's logical, analogical comparisons of form, function, and physiology of pterosaurs, birds, and reptiles as early as 1870. The bat-winged model was entirely consistent with the brilliant, unifying arguments of Owen's concepts of homology, the archetype, and methods of reasoning function and physiology from the principles of classification. But acceptance of this model had probably been cemented more than fifty years earlier by a single misidentification (Soemmerring 1817) and a picture evidently worth more than the arguments of Seeley, Zittel, and other firsthand observers of pterosaurs not affected by the same typological expectations.

Acknowledgments

For reading earlier drafts of this manuscript I would like to thank K. S. Thomson, J. H. Ostrom, J. A. W. Kirsch, J. D. Archibald, D. E. Schindel, A. J. de Ricqlès, S. P. Rachootin, S. Greenblatt, P. E. Olsen, and several anonymous reviewers. I would especially like to thank A. Desmond and S. J. Gould for helpful suggestions and encouragement. A. Pivorounas graciously helped translate some of the German passages. This work is based on portions of my Ph.D. dissertation at Yale University and was partially supported by National Science Foundation Doctoral Dissertation Improvement Grant DEB-780211.

Works Cited

Abel, O. 1925. *Geschichte und Methode der Rekonstruktion vorzeitlicher Wirbeltiere.* Stuttgart: Gustav Fischer Verlag.

Bramwell, C. D., and G. R. Whitfield. 1974. Biomechanics of *Pteranodon. Philosophical Transactions of the Royal Society of London* B 267: 503–81.

Buckland, W. 1836. *Geology and mineralogy, considered with reference to natural theology. Bridgewater treatises on the power, wisdom, and goodness of God as manifested in the creation.* Vol. 5. London.

Collini, C. 1784. Sur quelques zoolithes du Cabinet d'Histoire naturelle de S.A.S.E. Palatine et de Bavière, à Mannheim. *Acta Academia Theodoro-Palatinae, pars physica* 5: 58–103.

Coombs, W. J. 1975. Sauropod habits and habitats. *Palaeogeography, Palaeoclimatology, Palaeoecology* 17: 1–33.

Cope, E. D. 1869. Synopsis of the extinct Batrachia, Reptilia, and Aves of North America. *Transactions of the American Philosophical Society*, n.s. 14: 1–252.

Cox, C. B. 1980. Trimming the pterosaur's wings. *Nature* 284: 400–402.

Cuvier, G. 1801. Reptile volant: Extrait d'un ouvrage sur les espèces de quadrupèdes dont on a trouvé les ossemens dans l'intérieur de la terre. *Class. Sci., Math., et Phys. de l'Institute Nationale, du 26 brumaire de l'an 9.*

———. 1809. Mémoire sur le squelette fossile d'un reptile volant des environs d'Aichstedt, que quelques naturalistes ont pris pour un oiseau, et donc nous formons un genre de Sauriens, sous le nom de Ptero-Dactyle. *Annales, Musée d'Histoire naturelle* 13: 424.

———. 1812. *Recherches sur les animaux fossiles.* Paris.

———. 1834–36. *Recherches sur les ossemens fossiles.* 4th ed. Paris.

Desmond, A. J. 1975. *The hot-blooded dinosaurs: A revolution in paleontology.* London: Blond & Briggs.

———. 1979. Designing the dinosaur: Richard Owen's response to Robert Edmond Grant. *Isis* 70: 224–34.

———. 1982. *Archetypes and ancestors: Palaeontology in Victorian London, 1850–1875.* London: Muller.

Eaton, G. F. 1910. Osteology of *Pteranodon. Memoirs of the Connecticut Academy of Arts and Sciences* 2: 1–38.

Figuier, L. 1866. *La Terre avant le déluge.* 5th ed. Paris.

Goldfuss, A. 1831. Beiträge zur kenntnis verschiedener reptilien der Vorwelt. *Nova Acta Academia Leopoldina-Carolinae* (Breslau, Bonn) 15: 61–128.

Gombrich, E. H. 1961. *Art and illusion.* 2d ed. Princeton: Princeton University Press.

Hankin, E. H. 1913. *Animal flight.* London: Iliffe.

Hankin, E. H., and D. M. S. Watson. 1914. On the flight of pterodactyles. *Aeronautical Journal* 72: 1–12.

Hawkins, T. 1840. *The book of the great sea-dragons, Ichthyosauri and Pterosauri, Gedolim Taninim of Moses: Extinct monsters of the ancient earth.* London.

Heptonstall, W. B. 1971. An analysis of the flight of the Cretaceous pterodactyl *Pteranodon ingens*. *Scottish Journal of Geology* 7: 61–78.

Holst, E. von. 1957. Der saurierflug. *Paläontologische Zeitschrift* 31: 15–22.

Kermack, K. A. 1951. A note on the habits of the sauropods. *Annals and Magazine of Natural History* 12, no. 4: 830–23.

Kripp, F. von. 1943. Ein Lebensbild von *Pteranodon ingens* auf flugtechnischer Grundlage. *Nova Acta Leopoldina*, n.s. 12, no. 83: 217–46.

Marsh, O. C. 1882. The wings of pterodactyles. *American Journal of Science* 3, no. 16: 233.

Meyer, H. von. 1859–60. *Zur Fauna der Vorwelt, Vierte Abteilung: Reptilien aus dem lithographischen Schiefer des Jura in Deutschland und Frankreich.* Frankfurt.

Newman, E. 1843. Note on the pterodactyle tribe considered as marsupial bats. *The Zoologist* 1: 129–31.

Oken, L. 1819. *Pterodactylus longirostris*. *Isis von Oken* (Jena) 1819: 246.

Owen, R. 1842. Report on British fossil reptiles. Part 2. In *Reports of the Eleventh Meeting of the British Association for the Advancement of Science* 94–103. London, 1841.

———. 1848. *On the archetype and homologies of the vertebrate skeleton.* London.

———. 1858. *Monograph of the Fossil Reptilia of the Cretaceous Formations.* Supp. 1. London: Palaeontographical Society.

———. 1870. *A monograph of the fossil Reptilia of the Liassic Formations.* Pt. 3. London: Palaeontographical Society.

Padian, K. 1979. The wings of pterosaurs: A new look. *Discovery* 14: 20–29.

———. 1980. Studies of the structure, evolution, and flight of pterosaurs (Reptilia: Pterosauria). Ph.D. diss., Department of Biology, Yale University.

———. 1983a. Description and reconstruction of new material of *Dimorphodon macronyx* (Buckland) (Pterosauria: Rhamphorhynchoidea) in the Yale Peabody Museum. *Postilla* 189: 1–44.

———. 1983b. A functional analysis of flying and walking in pterosaurs. *Paleobiology* 9: 218–39.

———. 1985. On Richard Owen's archetype, homology, and the vertebral theory: Interrelations and implications. In *Abstracts of Papers, Seventeenth International Congress of the History of Science. Acts* 1: BJ.5P. Berkeley: Office for History of Science and Technology, University of California, Berkeley.

Pennycuick, C. 1972. *Animal flight.* London: Arnold.

Phillips, J. 1855. *Manual of geology: Practical and theoretical.* London: Griffin.

Riggs, E. S. 1904. Structure and relationships of opisthocoelian dinosaurs. Part II: The Brachiosauridae. *Field Columbian Museum, Geology* 2: 229–48.

Rudwick, M. J. S. 1964. The inference of function from structure in fossils. *British Journal of the Philosophy of Science* 15, no. 57: 27–40.

———. 1976a. *The meaning of fossils.* 2d. ed. New York: Science History Publications.

———. 1976b. The emergence of a visual language for geological science, 1760–1840. *History of Science* 14: 149–95.

Russell, E. S. 1916. *Form and function.* London: Murray.

Seeley, H. G. 1870a. *The Ornithosauria: An elementary study of the bones of Pterodactyles.* Cambridge: Cambridge University Press.

———. 1870b. Remarks on Prof. Owen's monograph on *Dimorphodon. Annals and Magazine of Natural History* ser. 4, 6: 129.

———. 1901. *Dragons of the air: An account of extinct flying reptiles.* London: Methuen.

Sneyd, A. D., M. S. Bundock, and D. Reid. 1982. Possible effects of wing flexibility on the aerodynamics of *Pteranodon. American Naturalist* 120: 455–77.

Soemmerring, S. Th., von. 1817. Über einen *Ornithocephalus brevirostris* der Vorwelt. *Denkschriften der königlinke Bayerische Akademie der Wissenschaften (math.-phys. Classe)* 6: 89–104.

Stein, R. S. 1975. Dynamic analysis of *Pteranodon ingens:* A reptilian adaptation to flight. *Journal of Paleontology* 49: 534–48.

Wagler, J. 1830. *Naturliches System der Amphibien.* Munich, Stuttgart, and Tübingen.

Watson, D. M. S. 1974. D. M. S. Watson's notes on pterodactyls (comment by C. D. Bramwell). *Philosophical Transactions of the Royal Society of London* B 267: 582.

Wellnhofer, P. 1978. *Pterosauria.* Handbuch der Paläoherpetologie, no. 19. Stuttgart: Gustav Fischer.

Wild, R. 1978. Die Flugsaurier (Reptilia, Pterosauria) aus der Oberen Trias von cene bei Bergamo, Italien. *Bolletino della Società Paleontologica Italiana* 17, no. 2: 176–256.

Williston, S. W. 1911. The wing-finger of *Pterodactylus*, with restoration of *Nyctosaurus. Journal of Geology* 19: 696–705.

Zittel, K. A. von. 1882. Über Flugsaurier aus dem lithographischen Schiefer Bayerns. *Paläontographica* 29: 47–80.

A REEVALUATION OF THE PLATE ARRANGEMENT ON STEGOSAURUS STENOPS

STEPHEN A. CZERKAS

T
he type specimen of Stegosaurus stenops *has been restudied with particular concern for the shape and placement of its ossicles, plates, and spikes. Evidence is given for reinterpreting the placement of plates in one single row.*

Since the discovery of stegosaur remains in 1877, the precise arrangement and interpretation of stegosaur plates and spikes has been an unresolved controversy for both paleontologists and artists attempting to reconstruct this popular but confusing dinosaur. An early restoration (Fig. 1) shows a single row of plates on the vertebral column followed by pairs of spikes. Since the turn of the century, the debate has centered upon two other opposing theories: whether the two rows of plates and spikes were arranged in pairs throughout the series, or arranged in two rows of staggered, alternating plates, followed by two pairs of matching tail spikes. Neither of these interpretations has gained unquestioned acceptance.

It is curious that the two contradictory concepts of paired or alternating plates in two rows were both originated in 1901 by Frederick A. Lucas, who based both of his interpretations on a remarkably well-preserved specimen of *Stegosaurus stenops* (National Museum of Natural History specimen, USNM 4934; Figs. 2–4). Initially, Charles R. Knight, under the direction of Lucas, portrayed a stegosaur (Lucas 1901) with plates arranged in pairs in two rows (Fig. 8). Subsequently George E. Roberts, again under Lucas's direction, portrayed a stegosaur with alternating plates in opposite rows (Fig. 9). Although Lucas may have preferred the alternating-plate concept, it is clear that he had his doubts: in his unpublished manuscript

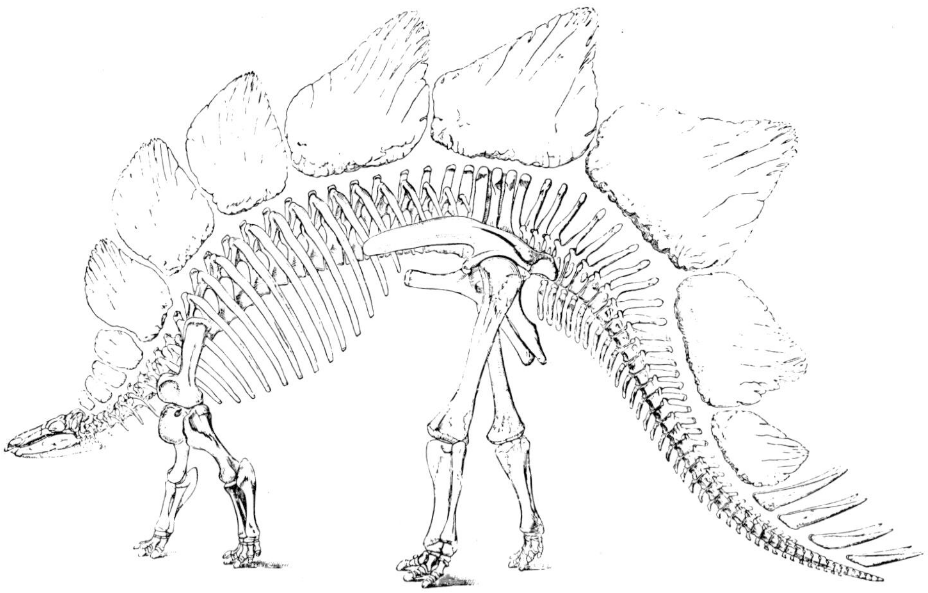

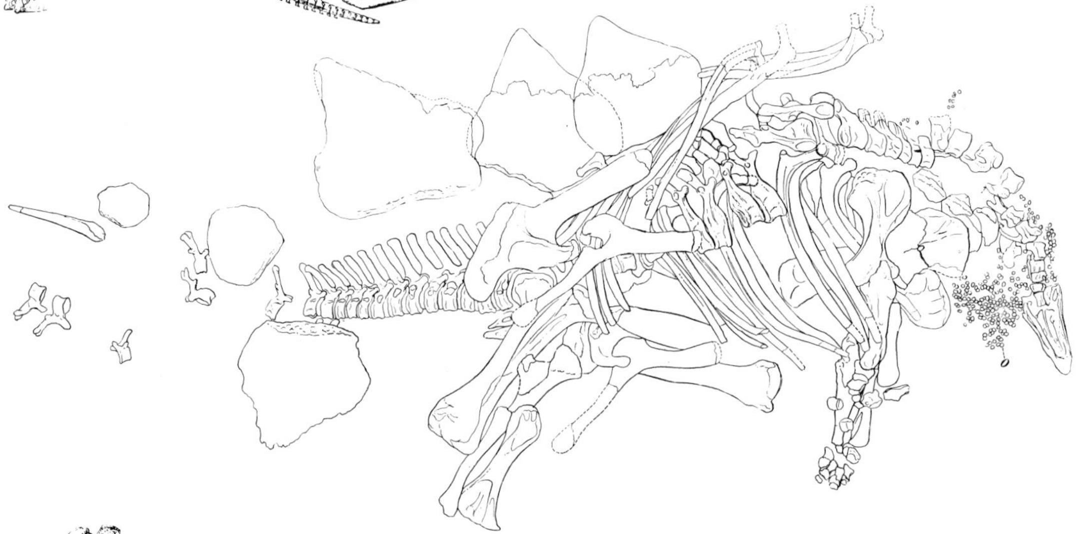

Figure 1. First reconstruction of *Stegosaurus* by O. C. Marsh (1891). There are only twelve plates, and they are arranged in a single median row. Marsh did not illustrate the pairing of the anterior plates, which he later described (Marsh 1896) and which would account for the four anterior plates not included. Plate 17 was not included to make room for the four extra tail spikes belonging to *S. ungulatus.* From Gilmore 1914: pl. 32.

Figure 2. Outline of the upper, or right, side of the skeleton of the *Stegosaurus stenops* specimen, USNM 4934; *O* indicates ossicles. The bones of the animal are shown just as they were found and are now exhibited. From Gilmore 1914: pl. 3.

Figure 3. View of the lower, or left, side of USNM 4934. This drawing shows the anterior plates as found. The ossicles (*O*) are incorrectly placed in this drawing (see Fig. 2, *O*, for their proper position). From Gilmore 1914: pl. 4.

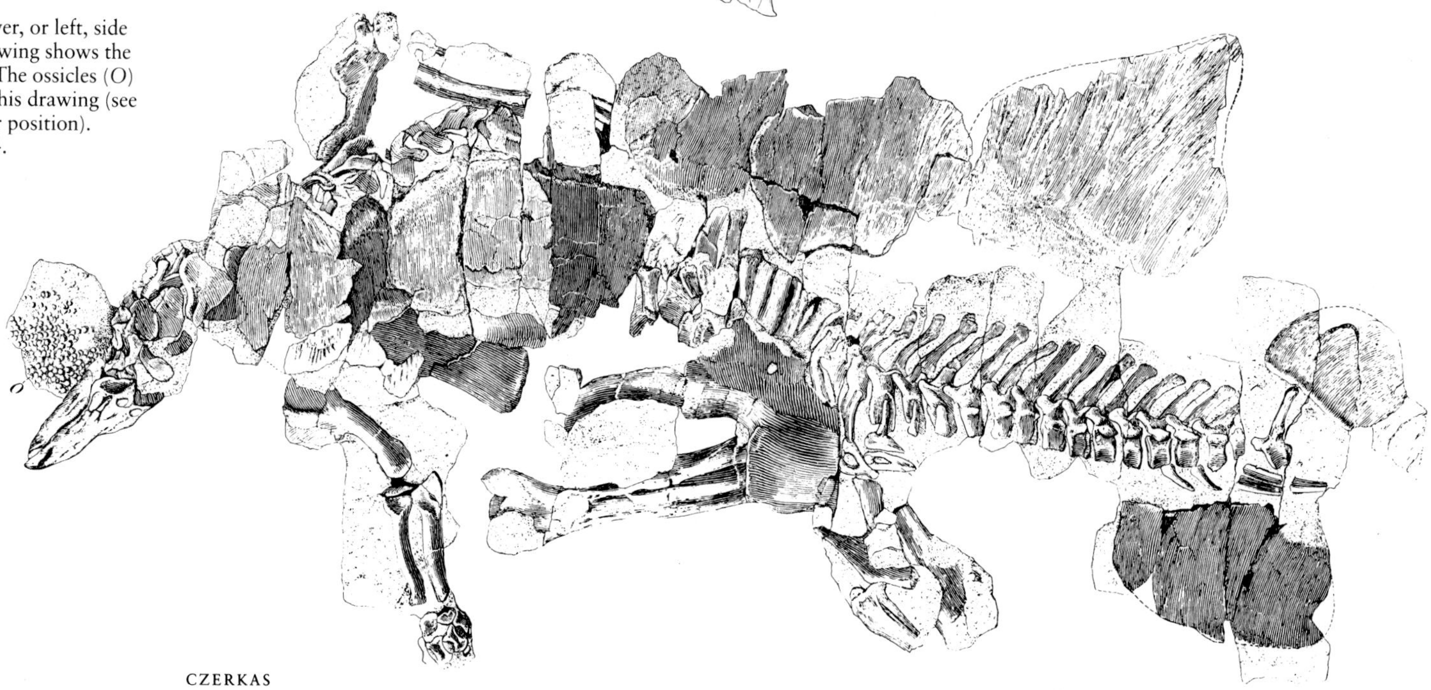

on stegosaurs he states that "the reader may draw his own conclusions as to how [the plates] were arranged in life" (Lucas circa 1900–1904). Referring to the alternating pattern, he noted that "this is merely a suggestion, and its confirmation or contradiction must depend on some future discovery."·

USNM 4934 is still the single most complete individual of any *Stegosaurus stenops* yet discovered. What is most important in the present context is that the dermal plates of this specimen were found in their proper sequence and relative positions. When he proposed the alternating-plate concept in 1901, Lucas cited as his evidence "first, that the plates did actually alternate as they lay embedded in the rock, and second, that no two of them were precisely similar in exact shape or dimensions" (Lucas circa 1900–1904).

Richard Swann Lull challenged the concept of alternating plates, stating that "no known reptile has alternating dermal elements" and also "that the position of the plates in the rock is hardly conclusive, for the series of one side might easily have shifted forward or backward during maceration or in the subsequent movement of the rocks." Lull continued: "The fact that each individual plate as shown above is in itself not symmetrical, indicates that the plates were not median but lateral structures and were arranged in at least two rows" (Lull 1910).

In this paper one of the earliest concepts, that of a single row of plates rather than two, is reexamined and reinterpreted as the solution to the mystery of the plates.

Many theories of plate arrangement were proposed by Prof. O. C. Marsh and others in the decades following the discovery of the first stegosaur, including recumbent plates (Marsh 1877), multiple rows of plates (Marsh 1880), and a single row of plates (Marsh 1887); some of these concepts were later

illustrated (Figs. 5–7). These early speculations were, however, based on very limited fossil remains.

After the discovery of *S. ungulatus*, Marsh was inundated from 1879 to 1887 with the greatest accumulation of stegosaurian remains ever discovered. This abundance of fossils came from the remarkable Quarry 13 of Como Bluff, Wyoming. This quarry was discovered by William H. Reed who worked the quarry for Marsh for over three years, after which J. L. Kenney continued work on the quarry during 1883. Kenney's major discovery in 1883 was of *S. sulcatus* (including its two distinctively robust spikes).

From 1884 to 1887, Fred Brown worked Quarry 13, carefully documenting the relative positions of all the bones as they were found, a vitally important practice largely ignored by many earlier collectors. The diagrams enable one to visualize the in situ placement of the semiarticulated and disarticulated remains of several individual stegosaurs, as well as the other dinosaurs found in the quarry. Even with the aid of Brown's diagrams, it is still difficult to identify the bones belonging to each individual, as the remains were often comingled and scattered. In any event, the Quarry 13 collection provided Marsh with a vast amount of information for interpreting the positions of plates and tail spikes. However, no specimen in Quarry 13 was more complete or better articulated than USNM 4934, the *Stegosaurus stenops* collected by M. P. Felch during 1885 and 1886 from Quarry 1 in Garden Park, Colorado. Marsh finally had before him the most complete and articulated stegosaur ever found.

Marsh (1891) published the first pictorial reconstruction of *S. ungulatus* (Fig. 1). In this drawing, the eight tail spikes are based on *S. ungulatus* (Peabody Museum of Natural History, Yale University, specimen, YPM 1853), but all of the

Figure 4. Series of dermal plates of USNM 4934 as viewed from the lower, or left, side (see Fig. 3). Plates 15, 16, and 17 are not shown. Drawn by G. E. Roberts in 1901 under the direction of F. A. Lucas and later published with additions in Gilmore's monograph (1914). Courtesy National Museum of Natural History, Smithsonian Institution.

plates are drawn from the *S. stenops,* USNM 4934. Only twelve plates are shown; they are in a single row with none in pairs or alternating. But in earlier and later papers (Marsh 1887, 1896) Marsh contradicted this skeletal reconstruction: "The upper portion of the neck, back of the skull, was protected by plates, *arranged in pairs* [italics added later in Lull 1910] on either side. These plates increased in size farther back, and thus the trunk was shielded from injury. From the pelvic region backward a series of huge plates stood upright along the median line, gradually diminishing in size to about the middle of the tail" (Marsh 1896). Contrary to his written descriptions, Marsh's skeletal reconstruction did not represent the plates *over the neck* in two rows of pairs, but did illustrate his original concept of one row for the *back half* of the animal. Recent discovery and examination of the original drawing reveals that the four plates over the neck representing the opposite row of paired plates were drawn in, accurately representing Marsh's written text, but for reasons unknown they were erased prior to publication. Because he had all the information from Quarry 13, and especially the *S. stenops,* USNM 4934, from Garden Park, it is important to consider why Marsh believed that some plates could rest on the midline but that the neck plates were paired. Why didn't Marsh place all of the

plates in pairs? The evidence for Marsh's interpretation was never cited in further detail.

When Marsh died in 1899 many of his specimens, including the *S. stenops* (USNM 4934) and most of the Quarry 13 material, were transferred to the United States National Museum.

In 1901, under Lucas's direction, USNM 4934 was reassembled and used as a basis for Knight's restoration of a stegosaur with two rows of paired plates (Fig. 8). At the same time, also under Lucas's direction, Roberts illustrated Plates 1 through 14 as they were found in situ (Fig. 4). Lucas then directed Roberts in a second life restoration, this time depicting two rows of alternating plates (Fig. 9). Thus, 1901 saw the genesis of both of the presently popular theories of plate arrangement. In 1903, Knight made a scale model of a stegosaur under the direction of Lucas that shows the plates in the alternating arrangement (Fig. 10). The tail spikes were reduced from the four pairs illustrated in Knight's earlier painting to two pairs.

When he left his position at the United States National Museum, Lucas left his unpublished manuscript (Lucas circa 1900–1904), which would strongly influence Charles W. Gilmore in his definitive monograph on *Stegosaurus* (Gilmore 1914).

Lull (1910) had the *S. ungulatus* mounted

for display with two rows of paired plates, almost half of which were plaster restorations of the "missing" mates to the actual bones. Lull did this to oppose Lucas's alternating-plate theory, using Marsh's reference to the paired cervical plates as the authority. But he paired all of the plates, disregarding the fact that Marsh had specifically retained his original single-row concept for the back half of the animal. Many plates have been found, and plates from two or more individual stegosaurs have been correlated, but I know of no identification of a matched pair from a single individual. USNM 4934 provided the plates in their proper sequence but failed to support Lull's theory as no two plates conclusively represented a matched pair. Despite the lack of supporting evidence, Lull's observation that "no known reptile has alternating dermal elements" cast considerable doubt on Lucas's staggered-plate theory.

Gilmore (1914) defended Lucas's theory of alternating plates and addressed plate arrangement in more detail than had any previous worker. Gilmore reviewed most of the existing restorations of *Stegosaurus*. He disregarded that significance of Marsh's skeletal reconstruction and revised description that depicted a single row of plates. It is evident that Gilmore was unconcerned as to Marsh's pairing of the cervical plates, as he failed

to mention this detail in his monograph. In fact, referring to a painting published by E. Ray Lankester (1905; see Fig. 11 herein), Gilmore failed to observe that the plate arrangement depicted by Lankester's artist closely followed Marsh's written description (1896). Gilmore saw "but little to commend" in this painting.

Gilmore apparently regarded Lull's paired-plate theory as the only valid argument against the alternating-plate theory. In support of his own argument for alternating plates, Gilmore (1914) quoted Lucas's reasoning: "First, that the plates did alternate as they lay embedded in the rock, and second, that no two of them were precisely similar in shape or dimensions." Gilmore argued convincingly that the two rows of plates did not shift post mortem into an alternating position, noting that "part of the series, as shown . . . has fallen to the left and lies under the body of the animal, while the posterior plates are approximately in the position above the pelvic region, yet both sections show the same alternating arrangement. . . . This exact spacing of the plates would indicate that they remained attached to the skin until becoming fixed in the position in which we now see them" (Gilmore 1914).

Gilmore (1914) modified Lull's original figures (Fig. 12a–c) of the placement of the cervical,

Figure 7. This life restoration by Frank Bond, 1899, depicts the armor plates as a recumbent, overlapping, scalelike carapace. The drawing, which was based on limited material, depicts a very idealized functional interpretation of plates and spikes. From Gilmore 1914: pl. 33.

Figure 8. Life restoration of *Stegosaurus ungulatus* by Knight, 1901, under the direction of Lucas. This was the first illustration showing plates in two rows, in this case paired. From Gilmore 1914: pl. 33. Courtesy American Museum of Natural History. See also pages xiii–ix.

dorsal, and caudal plates and the tail spikes by placing them higher and closer to the dinosaur midline (Fig. 12d–f). Gilmore stated that the bases of the cervical and anterior dorsal plates "appear to have overlapped the median line. . . . In other words, the expanded portion of the plates [the bases] of one row are in the center of the interspace of those on the opposite side, so that the point of where the plates emerged from the thick skin of the back must have been put very little off the middle line of the back." Gilmore, however, refused to actually interpret these plates as originating from the midline, as that would have kept him from accepting the concept of two rows existing in any position.

USNM 4934 lacks most of the caudal vertebrae, and Gilmore assumed that some of the plates of the tail region were also missing. Even though he correlated the last four caudal plates of USNM 4934 with those of another individual (USNM 4714), in which the plates were found in their proper sequence and only slightly displaced above an articulated tail (Fig. 13), he assumed that in both specimens the plates of the opposite rows were not preserved. Gilmore thus added from three to five extra caudal plates to represent the missing plates of the opposite row, raising the number in his complete series to twenty to twenty-two plates.

Over the years, Gilmore's monograph on *Stegosaurus* has remained the primary reference for stegosaur plate arrangement. The existence of two rows has been accepted by most paleontologists, but the concept of alternating plates is rarely accepted. Ironically, the one criticism stated by Lull "that no known reptile has alternating dermal elements" has been the factor by which so many paleontologists and artists have decided that Gilmore's evidence for two rows of alternating plates is incorrect. Gilmore never mentioned Lull's statement or challenged it by explanation. Perhaps he felt that the physical evidence he presented was enough to satisfy all doubts.

Gilmore's and Lull's interpretations suffer from a single major flaw: neither of them (or for that matter Lucas) gave sufficient consideration to Marsh's interpretation that the plates were situated in a single row. Gilmore (1914) noted that Marsh had formulated his interpretation "in accordance with the known position [of the plates] in *Stegosaurus stenops* [USNM 4934]." Gilmore then refuted Marsh's conclusions: "It will be observed that notwithstanding the positive evidence furnished by the *S. stenops* skeleton as to the existence of two parallel rows of fourteen dermal plates, Marsh placed the series in a single row of twelve along the median line." The "positive evidence" cited by Gilmore is that some of the plates are resting upon other plates. Gilmore's intent seems to have been to defend Lucas's opinion. Although Lucas was not dogmatic as to his beliefs, Gilmore had been placed in a position of defending the alternating pattern

Figure 11. Life restoration of *S. ungulatus* after E. Ray Lankester by an unknown artist, 1905. This painting follows Marsh's written description exactly in that it shows the anterior plates paired, followed by a single row of dorsal and caudal plates. From Gilmore 1914: pl. 35.

Figure 14. Gilmore's composite mount of
S. stenops. From Gilmore 1918.

Gilmore's addition of three to five extra caudal plates was necessary to represent the presumed existence of a second row of plates. That the last four caudal plates represent all of the plates of that region is demonstrated by the four caudal plates of specimen USNM 4714. Gilmore noted the similar positions of Plate 14 in both USNM 4934 and 4714 and also the similar measurements and general contours of each corresponding plate in the two specimens. Even with these two examples of specimens with only four caudal plates (and those of one specimen, USNM 4714, still in their proper sequence), Gilmore steadfastly defended the theory of two rows of alternating plates and ignored evidence for a single row of plates running down the midline. The assumption that USNM 4934 was incomplete and lacking in some of its tail plates further misled Gilmore.

The asymmetrical nature of the anterior plates would at first appear to be in conflict with Lull's statement that no known reptile has alternating dermal armor. However, he was referring mainly to the rows of dorsal scutes on crocodiles and gavials. In reptiles that possess a single, median row of dermal elements (e.g., *Cyclura cornuta*) it is not uncommon for the smaller, initially symmetrical dermal elements to develop asymmetry as they enlarge in growth, often alternating in opposing directions (Fig. 16). As it is fully possible for a single row of dermal elements to become alternating and asymmetrical in reptiles, it appears that this characteristic had developed in stegosaurs as well. A single row of midline dermal elements or ornamentation is not uncommon among dinosaurs and has also been found in the theropod *Ceratosaurus* (Gilmore 1920) and the hadrosaurs *Anatosaurus* (Osborn 1912), *Corythosaurus* (Brown 1916), and *Kritosaurus* (Parks 1920).

Several stegosaur individuals appear to have only four tail spikes, and *S. ungulatus* would be an unique exception if the eight tail spikes attributed to it are indeed from a single individual. The asymmetrical, oblique bases, the similar sizes, and the matching contours of opposing spikes are not conclusive evidence for two rows of paired spikes. The tail spikes may also have originated from the midline in one row, as adequate space is available.

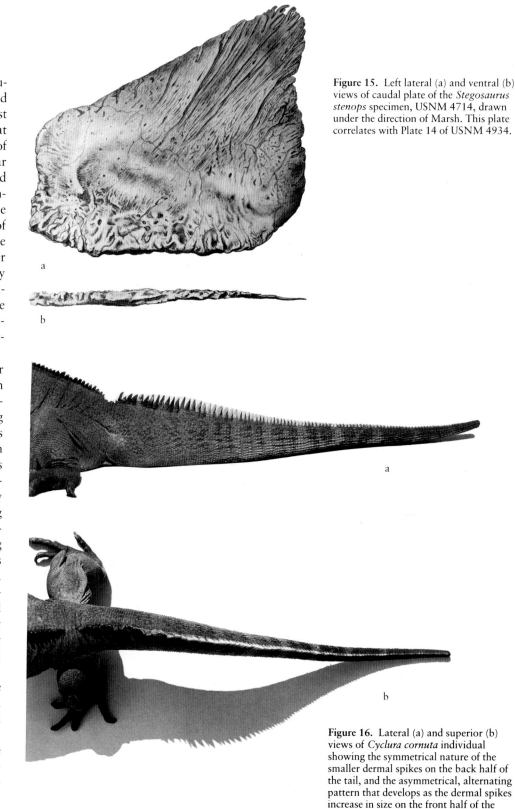

Figure 15. Left lateral (a) and ventral (b) views of caudal plate of the *Stegosaurus stenops* specimen, USNM 4714, drawn under the direction of Marsh. This plate correlates with Plate 14 of USNM 4934.

Figure 16. Lateral (a) and superior (b) views of *Cyclura cornuta* individual showing the symmetrical nature of the smaller dermal spikes on the back half of the tail, and the asymmetrical, alternating pattern that develops as the dermal spikes increase in size on the front half of the tail.

RTBakker
65

ing flies, mayflies, and aphids (Fig. 5).

There is not much diversity among freshwater invertebrates known at present (Russell 1964). Clam beds include thousands of specimens, generally representing only two or three different species. Recent study of these beds has shown that they may have other value. Some freshwater invertebrates are quite sensitive to environmental changes and can help determine the Cretaceous depositional environments. One site in Dinosaur Provincial Park displays a sequence of clam beds that were drowned by sand and mud, presumably carried by flood waters. Many of the clams died trying to dig out of the mud. The overlaying sands reveal that gas from the rotting bodies of the clams rose through the sediments. These types of sites can indicate the amount of sand accumulated in single flooding events.

More attention has been paid recently to isolated dinosaur bones. It is very difficult to walk far in any direction in Dinosaur Provincial Park without finding isolated bits of dinosaur bone, and millions of bones are exposed. If one attempted to collect all of these specimens, one would soon run out of space to store them. Although most are left in the field, it has been profitable to identify these isolated bits and pieces because approximately one percent of them are diagnostic enough to identify the species.

There are strong biases in Dinosaur Provincial Park against the preservation of small animals. Large skeletons stayed together after the animals died because of the greater weight of the bones and because of the strength of the soft tissues holding them together. Small specimens decomposed faster, were completely destroyed by scavengers, or were broken up by the action of the rivers. The net result is that very few animals weighing less than fifty kilograms are represented by articulated skeletons. By studying the isolated dinosaur bones, both baby dinosaurs and adults of small species have been recovered and identified.

The animals that lived in environments adjacent to stream beds had a greater chance of being buried and fossilized as complete skeletons than did animals that lived and died between the streams in forests, marshes, or other habitats. Many of the

Figure 4. Fossils collected by Barnum Brown for the American Museum were hauled out of the badlands of Alberta by horse-drawn wagon; photograph circa 1912. Specimens taken from the Drumheller and Dinosaur Provincial Park regions of Alberta by the early dinosaur hunters found their way into more than thirty-five institutions around the world.

Figure 5. Amber, which is abundant at several sites in Alberta, frequently contains the remains of spiders and insects. These aphids are among a line of twenty-seven preserved in an amber specimen 3 millimeters long.

Figure 6. This isolated braincase of Troödon, a small dinosaur (3 meters or less in length), was discovered in Dinosaur Provincial Park in 1982. Study of the specimen has revealed it to be very similar in general morphology to the braincases of modern birds.

OPPOSITE
Figure 3. *Barosaurus*, by Robert Bakker. Checklist 90.

small forms, such as *Troödon*, are almost entirely represented by isolated bones from the skull or skeleton. Comparison with articulated specimens of closely related species from Asia allows the identification of these forms and gives us a good idea of what the animals looked like. In 1982 the value of isolated bones was shown when a braincase of *Troödon* (Fig. 6) was discovered in Dinosaur Provincial Park. Study of this specimen showed that the braincase, including the well-preserved middle-ear region, of *Troödon* was very similar in general morphology to that of modern birds and emphasizes the fact that small carnivorous dinosaurs and birds are closely related (Currie 1985).

Over the past few years approximately one new dinosaur species has been discovered annually in Alberta, primarily on the basis of isolated bones. It is now known that some genera that were previously known only from the western United States or Asia were in fact living in Alberta as well. At one

Figure 8. *Centrosaurus* herd crossing a stream; restoration by Gregory Paul. Checklist 87.

OPPOSITE
Figure 7. *Kritosaurus incurvimanus*, by Vladimir Krb. This restoration is based on information obtained in the recovery of a specimen found entangled in the roots of a fossilized tree in Dinosaur Provincial Park. When the hadrosaur died seventy-five million years ago, its carcass floated downstream in a river until it came to rest against the tree at the bank. The dinosaur's skin left impressions in the mud under the body, which are preserved in the fossil rock. The upper part of the skeleton began to disarticulate as the body decomposed, and some of the bones were washed further downstream before becoming buried in the sand. Checklist 93.

Figure 12. Swimming ornithopod restoration by Gregory Paul. Trackways show that as some dinosaurs swam, they poled with their feet to change speed or direction. Courtesy Tyrrell Museum of Palaeontology.

Figure 13. Traveling ornithopods, a restoration by Gregory Paul suggested by a set of tracks showing at least ten ornithopods moving together in one direction. A portion of the trackway indicates that at one point one animal lurched sideways and bumped into a second, creating a domino effect of stumbling that involved four animals; the animals apparently then recovered and resumed their original course. Courtesy Tyrrell Museum of Palaeontology.

OPPOSITE
Figure 11. A restoration of *Styracosaurus albertensis*, the dinosaur occurring in the bone bed shown in Figure 9, by Vladimir Krb. Checklist 94.

THE LAST OF THE NORTH AMERICAN DINOSAURS

J. KEITH RIGBY, JR.

*S*ix localities have now produced Paleocene dinosaur remains, primarily teeth and more rarely bones, from screen-washed matrix obtained from the upper part of the Hell Creek Formation, McCone County, Montana. These fossils are thought to represent primary Paleocene deposition and are not derived from Cretaceous bank sources. Analysis of associated sediment, state of preservation, potential sources, and associated fauna and flora support such a conclusion. These studies also show that the last of the known North American dinosaurs survived the Cretaceous/Tertiary impact event in an environment typified by narrow riparian habitats separated by broad, open-canopy interfluves. The Hell Creek river channels were maintained by flash floods, which also served to concentrate vertebrate remains after very brief periods of transport. Vertebrate fossils closely associated with clay-pebble conglomerates probably represent extremely local faunal derivation.*

Few topics in paleontology create broader interest in the general public than the search for the ultimate cause of dinosaur extinction. Extraterrestrial causes recently advanced by several authors have again revived the discussion and heated the debate. Scientists are now combing the outcrops of late Cretaceous and early Tertiary rocks for clues that may hint at an answer to the question of dinosaur extinction. Some of these clues will reside in the deposits that produce the youngest known dinosaurs and should indicate changes in climate, vegetation, temperature, and general geography. These will be

Detail of "Dawn of a New Day" by Mark Hallett. Checklist 123.

119

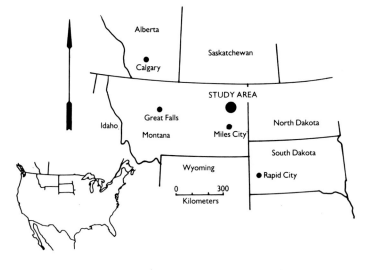

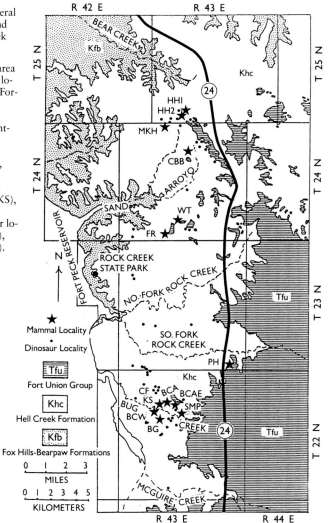

Figure 1. Index map showing the general location of the Fort Peck fossil field and the studied exposures of the Hell Creek Formation.

Figure 2. Geologic map of the study area showing fossil mammal and dinosaur localities of the Hell Creek and Tullock Formations along the east edge of the Big Dry Arm of the Fort Peck Reservoir, Montana. Localities are Bug Creek Anthills (BCA), Bug Creek Anthills East (BCAE), Bug Creek West (BCW), By George (BG), Chris's Bone Bed (CBB), Carnosaur Flat (CF), Ferguson Ranch (FR), Harbicht Hill One (HH1), Harbicht Hill Two (HH2), Ken's Saddle (KS), Not My Fault (NMF), Scmenge Point (SMP), and Wounded Toe (WT); other localities not shown are Big Bugger (BB), Fowl Error (FE), and Ken's Apex (KA).

key factors in understanding the biology of dinosaurs and potential causes of their extinction; they also will figure prominently in artistic restoration studies and education of the many who find dinosaurs so captivating.

Perhaps nowhere in the world is the final million years of dinosaur history more completely studied than in deposits of the Hell Creek Formation exposed along the eastern edge of the Big Dry Arm of the Fort Peck Reservoir in Montana's McCone and Garfield Counties. Field crews from the University of Minnesota, University of California, Berkeley, University of Notre Dame, University of California, Los Angeles, Brigham Young University, Colorado School of Mines, and elsewhere have been working in the Hell Creek Formation near the classic Bug Creek localities in east-central Montana (Figs. 1, 2). The Notre Dame crews and others have been studying the critical stratigraphic interval surrounding the Cretaceous/Tertiary (к/т) boundary. The Montana sequence is thought to be more nearly complete than most other boundary sections in North America. It certainly is much more complete than the section in the San Juan Basin of New Mexico and Colorado where one or more unconformities account for the loss of approximately five to seven million years of record, including the к/т boundary event (Fassett 1987; Brookins and Rigby 1987; Newman 1987; Rigby and Wolberg 1987; and others included in Fasset and Rigby 1987).

The extinction of dinosaurs has long been considered the definitive characteristic of the continental к/т boundary. L. Alvarez et al. (1980) and W. Alvarez et al. (1984) postulated that a large asteroid (or other extraterrestrial body) hit the earth and threw up a dust cloud that blanketed the earth for some time, blocked the sun's radiation, and dramatically reduced the earth's surface temperatures, resulting in the mass extinction of a variety of marine life forms in addition to the dinosaurs. The signature of this event is the abnormally high abundance in the impact-derived sediments of a rare heavy metal, iridium. Carl Orth of Los Alamos Laboratories has succeeded in locating a slight (ninety parts per billion) iridium concentration near what, based upon fossil-pollen studies (Orth in Sloan et al. 1986, Rigby et al. in press), is thought to be the K/T boundary in the Bug Creek area. The strong correlation of the pollen change, long used as a local terrestrial K/T boundary indicator, and the location of the iridium anomaly in both marine and terrestrial sections has been substantiated by a number of authors (Orth et al. 1981; Tschudy et al. 1984; and others). Nichols et al. (1986) have recently reconfirmed this exceptionally close association of iridium abundance and fossil-pollen change from Hell Creek equivalent beds in southernmost Saskatchewan, Canada (approximately 120 kilometers north of our study area).

Fossil-pollen studies, as well as the iridium concentrations noted by Orth, are indicators of the K/T boundary throughout our study area, in all three geologic sections studied to date. The boundary is marked by the disappearance of several fossil-pollen species, *Aquilapollenites* and *Proteacidites* among others (Fig. 3). Above the boundary there is a pronounced increase in spore abundance followed by the introduction of new pollen species typical of basal Tertiary (Paleocene) deposits (Nichols et al. 1986; Rigby et al. in press; Smit and van der Kaars, personal written communication 1985). All of these changes take place in the upper six meters of the Hell Creek Formation (six meters beneath the Z coal, the local stratigraphic boundary between the Hell Creek and Tullock Formations) exposed within the Bug Creek and Sand Arroyo 7.5-minute quadrangles.

The K/T boundary bed of the study area is a thin carbonaceous streak that contains resin globules and relatively abundant charcoal fragments up to one centimeter long. This suggests that the local K/T boundary is indeed marked by traces of a reasonably large wildfire like those recently suggested as having occurred at the K/T boundary by Wolbach, Lewis, and Anders (1985). The boundary fire does not, however, appear to have been any more severe than at least four other fire events that have been located in the upper part of the Hell Creek Formation and is observably less well developed than three of those events in the Bug Creek area. Each of these events is represented by a thin (one to ten centimeter thick) and locally thicker coal or carbonaceous stringer siltstone with locally abundant charcoal fragments. Thus, nearly all of the thin car-

Figure 3. Palynomorph zones of the uppermost Hell Creek Formation. Most palynomorph taxa continue through the K/T boundary interval; however, a few species, which form the extinction group, terminate at the interval where Orth located a slight iridium concentration ("The Event"). Immediately overlying this clay is sediment with a pronounced increase in fern spore abundance ("spore spike") and decreased pollen diversity. Above this, a group of "new" pollen taxa characteristic of earliest Paleocene deposits appear (Nichols et al. 1986; Rigby et al., in press).

bonaceous "streaks" in the upper part of the Hell Creek Formation reported by various authors may represent wildfire events and paleosols.

PALEOCENE DINOSAURS

The youngest Hell Creek dinosaurs occur in channel infillings in the uppermost part of the formation (Rigby 1985; Rigby and Sloan 1985). These channel deposits are Paleocene in age on the basis of contained fossil pollen and on stratigraphic evidence that shows truncation of beds containing a weak iridium event (ninety parts per billion) and the very real fossil-pollen change described above. Six localities have produced dinosaur remains from channel deposits known to be of Paleocene age: Bug Creek West (BCW), Scmenge Point (SMP), Harbicht Hill (HH), Harbicht Hill-Two (HH2), Ferguson Ranch (FR), and Wounded Toe (WT; see Fig. 2). There is little doubt that dinosaur fossils, primarily teeth, actually occur in Paleocene deposits. In a joint research project in progress, P. J. Currie, R. E. Sloan, and I are investigating the possibilities of using dental characters to recognize dinosaurian taxa; we have had some success (Sloan et al. 1986). Certain higher taxonomic groups of dinosaurs can be recognized on the basis of their dentition. These

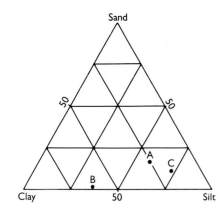

Figure 4. Grain-size distributions of sediment samples used in flume experiments (redrawn from Smith 1972). Sediment A is a commercial mixture of fine sand, silt, and dominantly kaolinite and illite. Sediment B consists primarily of silt and illite and was obtained in a saturated state from a southern California mountain stream. Sediment C, collected in a compacted state, is a Pleistocene mixture of fine quartz sand, silt, and primarily illitic mud that is eighteen percent calcium carbonate by weight.

groups and their relative dental abundance are listed in Table 1. Creating a faunal list solely on the basis of dinosaurian dental characters is premature.

There is a possibility that the dinosaur teeth represent reworked fossils derived from Cretaceous bank material. If this were the case, the following occurrence phenomena would have to be explained.

Clay-pebble conglomerates. Fossil vertebrates, including remains of the last of the dinosaurs, occur concentrated in matrix-supported, clay-pebble conglomerates within the Hell Creek Formation. They are not randomly scattered throughout any fluvial sand body, nor are they found in any abundance in channel-lag deposits lining the channel floor or in known bank-failure deposits. Their occurrence appears to be primarily independent of at least these known contamination mechanisms.

Smith (1972) conducted flume transport studies on clay-silt clasts that were much like those clasts found associated with the vertebrates of the Hell Creek Formation. In his study three types of uniform-sized "mud" clasts (3 by 3 by 0.5 centimeters; see Fig. 4) with variable water content were subjected to steady water flow at sixty centimeters per second and twenty-five centimeters per second over a sand-impregnated or rough flume bottom. At no time was sediment coarser than the silt and clay originally contained in the clasts introduced into the flume. Periodic measurements of sediment in suspension were made to determine sediment remaining as clasts. Each experiment set was allowed to continue uninterrupted until all of the clasts were disaggregated and the sediment was held in suspension.

The study basically showed that clay-silt clasts like those of the Hell Creek Formation had a remarkably short survival time. A water transport speed of sixty centimeters per second was just fast enough to cause intermittent clast transport through the flume. Erosive forces, therefore, had two sources: the shearing effects of the moving water and the rough-bottom impact. Most low clasts with water content disintegrated within a few minutes of initiation of the run, but some samples with water contents of thirty-six percent were able to survive no more than eighty minutes of the run

before totally disintegrating (Fig. 5). In other words, no clay clast was able to survive a transport of more than 3.03 kilometers. In all probability actual transport distance of clay-silt clasts in the Hell Creek Formation is much less than this figure: during the eighty-minute experimental run of the longest-lasting clasts transport was only intermittent, and Hell Creek channel deposits contain a substantial amount of medium-grained sand that would have led to more rapid abrasion than seen in the flume experiments. A realistic transport distance for Hell Creek clay-silt clasts of approximately the same size as those used in the flume studies would have been perhaps between one and two kilometers.

The study also analyzed deterioration of clasts when subjected to running water at a velocity of twenty-five centimeters per second. The speed was not sufficient to cause transport, but the lower water speed did succeed in increasing the survival time of clasts from just a few minutes in some transport cases to a maximum of six days (Fig. 5). In both velocity cases survival time seems to be enhanced by increased water content and the higher clay-to-silt ratio.

These studies show that, regardless of the source of the clay-pebbles in the Hell Creek channel deposits, clasts that form the major bulk of the vertebrate-producing clay-pebble conglomerate cannot survive transport over even limited distances, nor can they survive extended exposure to running water, even without the coarser clastic material certain to be present in Hell Creek streams. In other words, the clay-pebble conglomerates must have had an exceptionally local derivation.

There is a very high correlation between fossil vertebrate occurrences and distribution of clay-pebble conglomerates. Rare overbank concentrations of vertebrates, primarily dinosaurs, have been found (Fig. 2), but rarely do they consist of more than the partial remains of a single individual and the shed teeth of carnivores who may have fed on the carcass. The overwhelming majority of fossil vertebrate localities in the Hell Creek Formation is associated with channel deposits, and the fossils are invariably concentrated in a clay-pebble conglomerate. Whatever forces are forming the nonbank failure clay-pebble conglomerates are also concentrating fossil vertebrates.

Potential sources of vertebrates. There is little doubt that the youngest known dinosaurs in Hell Creek Formation occur in channel infillings of Paleocene age. Since these channel deposits truncate beds of Cretaceous age, is it possible that these youngest dinosaurs could be eroded free from Cretaceous sediment and later concentrated in Paleocene clay-pebble conglomerates?

Based upon the survivability of clay-pebble conglomerates and the highly correlated codeposition of clay pebbles and vertebrate remains, it seems very probable that whatever vertebrate remains are found must have been derived from local sources, perhaps within a radius of three kilometers or less. Two sources of such derivation are acknowledged: surface, channel, and floodplain introduction during periods of peak flow and bank erosion.

Located within the clay-pebble conglomerates and codepositionally associated with the vertebrates in question are a number of remains that would be virtually impossible to introduce into the stream by bank failure mechanisms. These remains include leaves and cones from taxodeaceous trees; reasonably complete, high-spired gastropod shells; complete (carapace and plastron) turtle shells; unabraded fish and turtle suture joints with the complete, ragged edge exposed; delicate mammal jaws with teeth intact; and vertebrae of various forms with spines and processes complete and intact (Fig. 6). These same types of fossils do not appear in other types of clay-pebble conglomerates (such as bank-failure deposits) and are found only on the most rare occasions in channel-lag sequences nor do they appear when clay-silt clasts from such deposits are experimentally screen-washed (McKenna 1965).

We have checked to see if, in the most protected nooks and crannies of collected vertebrates (such as the interiors of turtle skulls or bases of unresorbed crocodile tooth roots), any traces of bank sediment, rather than channel sediment, could be found. Since these forms were not transported far and generally were the least abraded of the materials collected, not all original burial sediment should have been removed by what little transport had occurred. No bank sediment was found in any of the more than fifty items examined, which strongly suggests a source other than bank failure for most of the concentrated vertebrates.

If these fossil vertebrates were locally derived, as association with the clay pebbles would suggest, then the bank abundance of vertebrates must be assessed to see if bank materials are sufficiently abundant to account for concentrations seen in channel sequences. Sloan et al. (1986, here modified) detailed the results of the University of Notre Dame and University of Minnesota screen-washing projects and the Milwaukee Public Museum's Dig-a-Dinosaur project in which substantial areas of Hell Creek exposure in the Bug Creek area have been surface prospected. These studies (Table 1) show a general decline in abundance of dinosaur materials as evidenced by the decline in the number of dinosaur teeth per metric ton of clay-pebble conglomerate screened and in the observed surface abundance in all types of sedimentary environments as one stratigraphically approaches and crosses the K/T boundary. This same decline is seen in the abundance and type of dinosaur remains (pri-

TABLE 1. DINOSAUR TOOTH ABUNDANCE IN COLLECTIONS FROM SCREEN-WASHED MATRIX, HELL CREEK FORMATION, MONTANA[1]

| | Cretaceous | | | | Paleocene | | |
| | | | BCA | | | | |
	CF	KS	Low	High	BCW/SMP	HH	FR
Tyrannosaurid	1	2				1	
Albertosaurid	45	6	1	3	5	1	1
Ceratopsian	45	141	110	35	75	113	59
Hadrosaurian	12	142	627	88	110	40	143
Ornith. indet.	26	55		3	6	3	
Small theropod	23	100	32	48	40	5	54
Total teeth	152	446	784	158	241	163	257
Metric tons screened	0.73	2.18	11.66	4.73	10.27	5.27	11.64
Teeth/ton	208.2	204.6	67.2	33.4	23.5	30.9	22.1

1. Localities are Carnosaur Flat (CF), Ken's Saddle (KS), Bug Creek Area (BCA), Scmenge Point (SMP), Harbicht Hill (HH), and Ferguson Ranch (FR). Dinosaur tooth abundances for each of the stratigraphically organized localities are grouped by higher taxonomic group. Data presented are derived from University of Notre Dame 1982–1984 collections (except those for HH, which are from University of Minnesota). Using dental elements for dinosaur taxonomy is a new procedure that may be useful when further refined. Taxonomic groups show the unique character of most localities; relative taxon abundance shows that larger dinosaur teeth occur independent of sediment sorting.

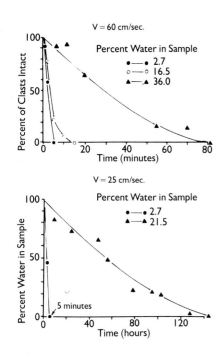

V = 60 cm/sec.

Percent Water in Sample
● — ● 2.7
○ — ○ 16.5
▲ — ▲ 36.0

V = 25 cm/sec.

Percent Water in Sample
● — ● 2.7
▲ — ▲ 21.5

Figure 5. Survivability of clasts of Sediment B (Fig. 4) in flume studies (modified from Smith 1972). Type B clasts were consistently the most durable in both water velocities tested, and the samples with the highest water content survived the longest of all clasts tested.

marily teeth) that we have collected in large screen-washed samples from several localities concentrated in the uppermost part of the Hell Creek Formation.

In the Hell Creek Formation of the study area, fossil vertebrates weather to a powdery pale gray, and even the smallest remains can be seen at distances of five to ten meters. Fragments of individual hadrosaur tooth plates (0.6 by 0.8 centimeters) were observed at distances of up to six meters. Even the smallest of medium-sized vertebrate remains can be spotted in the drab gray and green overbank shales through which the Paleocene streams cut their channels. Several prospecting expeditions have attempted to locate vertebrates in the shale and mudstone associated with the channel sequences, with at best marginal success. One or two scraps of bone or an isolated tooth plate can be recovered by one person during each work day. Even these remains may be slope washed to the discovery site from overlying channel sequences where they occur more abundantly. Fossil vertebrates are simply not common in the overbank deposits and, in fact, are so rare that to derive major vertebrate concentrations from bank deposits is highly unlikely.

The distribution of ceratopsian skulls and postcrania gives further evidence as to the type of depositional environment seen in the upper part of the Hell Creek Formation. Rarely does one find postcranial material associated with the reasonably common ceratopsian skulls located in overbank deposits; most dinosaurian postcranial elements occur in channel deposits. The skulls occur as isolated elements in crevasse-splay silts and overbank muds and silts. Because of their large size they remain behind, while other elements are swept away during periods of peak river flow and become incorporated into channel deposits. It appears that the flood plains are periodically swept and available surface materials are concentrated in channel-fill deposits. The overbank appears depopulated, while the channel vertebrate abundance appears exaggerated.

The distribution of vertebrate remains within screen-washed collections may offer additional information about the potential for rework-

ing. Bulk samples of clay-pebble conglomerate have been screened, and the resulting sediment concentrates sorted to remove identifiable vertebrate remains. Some localities, like Carnosaur Flat (CF) (Table 1), produce carnosaur teeth in unusual abundance (more than fifty percent of the total collection), while most localities throughout the Hell Creek and Judith River Formations produce the same taxa but at about five percent or less. The relative proportion of hadrosaur to ceratopsian teeth also varies widely between localities and appears to be independent of any sedimentological sorting (based on comparison of relative size and abundance of other faunal elements held in common by all localities, such as gar scales). If there were to be any appreciable reworking of vertebrate material, the reworking would make collections more homogeneous and would certainly eradicate pronounced differences such as those found at Carnosaur Flat.

Not only does it appear that reworking has had minimal influence on the vertebrate concentrations, but the distribution patterns in screen-washed collections and the short transport distances of the clay pebbles suggest that dinosaurian types may have been very territorial in their behavior, such that differences in dinosaur populations are preserved on a scale of three to five kilometers. Alternatively if these clay-pebble concentrations of vertebrates represent essentially instantaneous samples of the nearby extant fauna, faunal differences could be explained as seasonal features or, in an extreme interpretation, as indicative of herding behavior patterns.

Transport abrasion. Reworked materials generally appear more abraded than those that have suffered limited transport. It might be possible to look at dinosaurian remains in Paleocene deposits and determine if abrasion features suggest more damage than that suffered by other faunal elements.

Most dinosaurian fossils recovered from screen-washed samples consist of shed teeth. One of the most susceptible features of such teeth to abrasion would be the thin, sharp edge formed by the resorption of dentine prior to loss of the tooth. Shed deciduous teeth (milk teeth) of mammals can

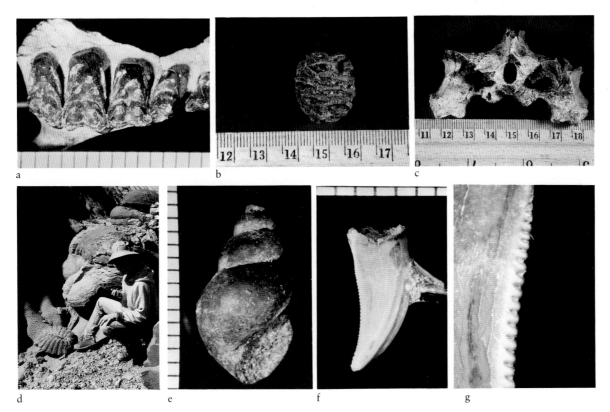

be easily recognized in collections and compared. Naturally shed mammalian and reptilian teeth from living organisms were compared to see if there were differences in the nature of the sharp shed edge between the two groups; none was found. The same sharp resorption edge is retained in both groups. Fossil samples were also analyzed to see if these edges were retained. Not all teeth of the mammals and crocodiles studied retained the sharp edge; a large proportion of the more than four thousand crocodile teeth, however, retained the edge as did a high percentage of mammal milk teeth.

Collected dinosaur teeth retained the resorption edge in a consistently better state of preservation than did crocodile teeth and in about the same state as shed mammal milk teeth. Not all dinosaur teeth preserved the edge in a pristine condition. In each sampled locality, however, a substantial number retained the shed edge in a very nearly pristine condition. In many cases these were the smallest teeth, those most subject to transport. Many teeth from Paleocene collections also re-

tained delicate rugose features of the enamel, serrations on carnosaur teeth, and parallel scratches in occlusal wear facets that would certainly have been immediately lost during transport for any distance or much exposure to traction or saltation abrasion due to bed-load sediment transport.

Comparisons of "Paleocene" dinosaur teeth were made with collections derived from unquestioned Cretaceous deposits to see if any noticeable differences in abrasion features could be seen; none was found. If the dinosaur teeth were reworked, at least the same reworking processes had to similarly function in Cretaceous and Paleocene deposits.

A variety of bone types, including those of dinosaurs, from all localities studied produced elements with eroded features in varying proportions. Some turtle plates are sufficiently rounded to have lost most of the ragged suture joint and some surface ornamentation; *Champsosaurus* vertebrae have lost most of their dense bone exterior; small-vertebrate limb elements have lost their articular ends; and in extreme cases dinosaur frill and limb

Figure 6. Examples of fossils that would be difficult to rework from Cretaceous into Tertiary sediments. a. Maxilla of *Protungulatum donnae* from the Bug Creek Anthills. b. Taxodeaceous cone from Bug Creek West. c. Posterior view of a turtle skull from Bug Creek West. d. Complete turtle shell (carapace and plastron) from a channel sandstone just beneath Bug Creek West. e. High-spired gastropod steinkern from Ken's Saddle. f. Small carnivorous dinosaur tooth, which shows the fragile shed edge at its base complete with the slight discoloration seen in shed modern crocodile teeth (Ferguson Ranch). g. Same dinosaur tooth (Fig. f) with the posterior margin enlarged to show the faint scratches in the enamel created during mastication while the animal was alive; such features would certainly disappear during minimal transport and abrasion (Ferguson Ranch).

elements are preserved as lumps of spongy bone as at Chris's Bone Bed (CBB) (Lupton, Gabriel, and West 1980).

Most of the vertebrate fossil mass is assumed to have been transported some distance, however small. Studies of the Bug Creek Anthills (BCA), where sedimentologic relationships are best exposed, have been conducted. Several scour-and-fill structures have been observed within the BCA main fossil quarry face, allowing us to sequence depositional events. It is not as yet known if the sequence studied represents scour structures of a single depositional event caused by minor current variations or separate depositional events separated by weeks to years. Virtually all of the lenticular deposit forming BCA consists of matrix-supported, gray-green, silty, clay-pebble conglomerates, clay-cemented, fine- to medium-grained sandstones, and angular bank-failure blocks. Two screen-washed samples have been collected, one from the bottom 1.5 meters and the other from essentially 1.5–3.0 meters above the bottom of the deposit. This upper interval is the one from which virtually all other BCA collections have been made.

Early in our investigations we recognized that the size and abundance of clay pebbles decrease toward the top of the deposit. Was the distribution of fossil vertebrates similarly graded? Comparison of the two screen-washed samples produced identical vertebrate faunal lists, but the proportional distribution of faunal elements varied. The bottom sample was enriched in the abundance of *Protungulatum* and large multituberculate and dinosaur teeth. The lower sample contained approximately seventy dinosaur teeth per metric ton of matrix screened, while the upper sample produced twenty-seven to thirty teeth per metric ton (Sloan et al. 1986).

Although very difficult to quantify in absolute terms, the surprising observation was that abrasion characteristics of all vertebrate-faunal elements increased upward in the section, corresponding to the decrease in size and abundance of the uniform gray-green silty clay pebble. The total amount of mammal teeth recovered per metric ton of sediment processed, regardless of size, was higher in the upper sample, and more of them showed the effects of abrasion. It appears as though the same long-channel clay-pebble deposit was itself being transported and sequentially stacked downstream. Such a situation was observed in a clay-pebble deposit in the main channel of present-day Bug Creek (Figs. 7, 8). Clay pebbles were derived from desiccation-cracked channel-bottom silts and muds near a nick point and were transported downstream for about fifty meters. Scour-and-fill structures were first noticed at about half the distance downstream; near the termination, five superposed scour-and-fill structures could be seen in a deposit that was never more than twenty-five centimeters thick. If this model is true for the larger scale Hell Creek clay-pebble conglomerates, as reduction in size of mammal teeth, dinosaur tooth abundance and clay pebbles would indicate, then most of the abrasion seen in collected specimens must have occurred within a relatively short transport distance.

Many of the specimens display asymmetrical abrasion. Some mammal jaws are unabraded on one side, yet so deeply abraded on the other that the molar roots are exposed along their entire length. Some mammal and dinosaur teeth are deeply eroded and pitted on one side and virtually unabraded on the other. Multituberculate blades commonly show more abrasion on one side than the other while preserving a "pristine" upper profile with all serrations and cusps intact. It seems quite probable that much of the abrasion seen in Hell Creek screen-washed collections cannot have been achieved by much transport of the vertebrate materials. More probably these fossils remained on the floor of the channel for some time, were subjected to traction abrasion and abrasion from the saltation load of the stream, and then were deposited in clay-pebble conglomerates. Certainly they could not have been transported far because the likelihood of symmetrical abrasion increases with increased transport distance.

FAUNAL SELECTIVITY

If reworking of Cretaceous deposits is to produce a fossil contribution to younger Paleocene sediments, then a large part of the entire Cretaceous fauna, and not just the dinosaurs, should appear in Paleocene channel infillings. The work of a number of authors

(summarized by Archibald 1982) has revealed some basic mammalian faunal succession (Fig. 9). Analyses of minimum numbers of individuals present reveal that, even in deposits as old as the lower and middle Hell Creek, mammals outnumber dinosaurs, and their dominance and diversity increases as one approaches and crosses the K/T boundary. If Cretaceous vertebrate faunas were reworked into Paleocene channel sandstones, then a major part of these older faunas should also appear and not just the dinosaurs (Fig. 9). The most common elements, Cretaceous mammals, should certainly appear. Many mammals common in Cretaceous sediments (many species of *Alphadon, Cimolestes, Pediomys*) do not appear in the younger deposits. There are no known mechanisms for reworking only the dinosaur material and leaving behind other, commoner elements.

Rapidly evolving ungulate mammals that are known to have differentiated during this interval of time also do not appear in mixed mammal assemblages. Perhaps the best example of this phenomenon is found in the evolution of ungulate mammals. One ungulate species, *Protungulatum donnae*, is found in BCA with eight species ultimately being found at FR (Sloan et al. 1986). In cases where two channel deposits with different ungulate mammal content intersect (Fig. 10), the younger eroding the older (BCA eroding KS; BG eroding the stratigraphic interval including KS, BCA, and BCW), the mammal faunas do not mix. The taxa held in common are sufficiently different to recognize the two populations as statistically distinct. Also, only weak sedimentological sorting between locations has been observed (BCA case cited earlier). All localities contain small (two millimeter) mammal teeth as well as large dinosaur teeth (one centimeter and larger). Mammal faunas can be shown not to mix in channel-to-channel erosion, the most optimal contitions for doing so. How then are the dinosaurs to mix and become incorporated into Paleocene sediments yet leave the more abundant Cretaceous mammalian faunal elements behind?

It seems highly probable that Paleocene dinosaur faunas of the Fort Peck fossil field do not represent reworked samples. Therefore, dinosaurs almost certainly survived the K/T asteroid impact well into the Paleocene where their numbers continued to decline until extinction in Montana was achieved, a minimum of 40 thousand years (based on average Hell Creek sedimentation rates) to perhaps a maximum of 250 thousand years after the impact event (assuming the presence of an unconformity at the Hell Creek/Tullock formational boundary at the base of the upper z coal).

Figure 7. Modern Bug Creek channel. Clast-supported clay-pebble conglomerates can be seen along the left margin of the channel; these extend from the nick point just out of view in the foreground to about midway around the next meander bend. The conglomerates are massive and thickest for about thirty meters below the nick point, but toward the downstream end of the deposit several scour-and-fill structures can be seen in superposition.

Figure 8. Clay-pebble conglomerates of the Modern Bug Creek. This is the thickest part (twenty-five centimeters) of the linear, bank margin clay-pebble lens. Individual clasts are made of clay-cemented siltstones with coal flecks—the identical material that makes up the desiccated surface on top of the clay pebbles and that makes up the silts on the channel floor. The clay pebbles are certainly derived from either or both of these exceptionally local sources.

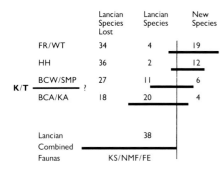

	Lancian Species Lost	Lancian Species	New Species
FR/WT	34	4	19
HH	36	2	12
BCW/SMP	27	11	6
BCA/KA	18	20	4
Lancian Combined Faunas			38
KS/NMF/FE			

K/T ——— ?

Figure 9. Stratigraphic distribution of fossil mammal species. Localities (at left; see Fig. 2 for full names and geographic location) are organized in relative stratigraphic order. The probable Cretaceous-Tertiary (K/T) boundary is drawn between BCA and BCW. Lancian (unquestionably Cretaceous) mammalian faunas have approximately thirty-eight species and are known from a reasonably wide sampling area over western North America. Twenty of these species are present in BCA, and the number declines as one crosses the K/T boundary. There does not appear to have been a radical mammalian extinction event nor are there a large number of Cretaceous mammals species present in Paleocene localities (i.e., HH and FR) that contain dinosaurs.

ENVIRONMENT OF THE LAST OF THE DINOSAURS

If the asteroid was not the cause of dinosaur extinction, what was the ultimate cause?

The answer must lie in more gradual causes than in extraterrestrial impact events. Evidence supporting such an event, however, is substantial (Smit and Klaver 1981; Orth et al. 1982; W. Alvarez et al. 1984; Bohor et al. 1984; Nichols et al. 1986, among others). I am reasonably certain that there was such an impact, but the biological consequences of such an event are much debated. Some tantalizing clues relevant to an ultimate explanation of dinosaur extinction are now being investigated. Some deal with interpretations of local paleoenvironmental conditions in Montana, which may imply global phenomena.

Virtually all of the Hell Creek vertebrates screen-washed from localities in the study area are found in matrix-supported clay-pebble conglomerates. Flume studies (Smith 1972) have shown that reasonably large clay-silt clasts can be moved with water velocity of sixty centimeters per second. Much higher speeds and induced turbulence, perhaps bordering on mudflow conditions, however, would be needed to produce the type of clay-pebble conglomerate seen in most of our vertebrate sites. Stream flow of 1.5 meters per second is typically recorded in the Mississippi River from Saint Louis, Missouri, to Vicksburg, Mississippi (Leopold and Maddock 1953). Such speeds, fluid viscosity, and other parameters are not sufficient to produce nonbank-failure clay-silt clast conglomerates. Most Hell Creek channel-fill clay pebbles are unusual in that they are flat, are of a uniform silty texture and color, can be generally separated from clay-rich bank-failure clay pebbles, and can only survive a very limited amount of transport. By comparison with known environments, like present-day Bug Creek, it can be assumed that our fossils were deposited in rivers during periods of peak flash discharge. These river systems probably derived most of their clay-pebble content from nearby desiccated bottom mud and silt.

These channels were not totally dry periodically, as evidenced by the common aquatic elements of the fauna (Estes and Berberian 1970), yet clay-pebble conglomerates strongly suggest that at least part of the channel floor was dried. Could standing pools, supplied by subsurface stream flow, function as water holes to concentrate the vertebrate fauna by providing a water source during dry periods? The famous BCA site is probably derived from just such a situation.

It has long been assumed that the vertebrate abundance at BCA was produced by the concentration of carnivore scat, which had been periodically swept from the floodplain surface over a long period of time. Bone and teeth residues would have been concentrated in channel bottoms, the local low drainage points, to appear later in clay-pebble conglomerates. This scenario may not be totally correct. For example, one of the most common BCA mammals is *Protungulatum donnae*. The number of shed milk teeth of this species collected in screen-washed concentrates is about sixty-five to seventy-five percent of the minimum number of adult individuals. The presence of such a high percentage of shed milk teeth would argue against a carnivore concentrate; at least the youngsters were alive when they lost their baby teeth. Such an abundance would suggest a place nearby where the animals came to drink and/or spend a large part of their time. Furthermore, the collection contains a large number of foot bones in proportion to other postcranial elements, and may be indicative of water-hole conditions as Behrensmeyer and Boaz (1980) suggest. The question then, at least for BCA, is how did such a phenomenal concentration of vertebrate material (eight mammal teeth per kilogram; Sloan and Van Valen 1965) build up without lengthy transport or reworking. The water hole located slightly upstream from the BCA main quarry with its massive clay-pebble conglomerates seems to be the best explanation.

Stream-bank geometry offers another significant clue to environmental conditions. Flow-maintained channels in relatively moist environments of low regional relief tend to have gently sloping banks (Fig. 11), while flood-maintained channels of dryer climates tend to have steep banks characteristic of large-scale bank failure or collapse. What we see in the Bug Creek area, particularly among the youngest channels of the Hell

Creek, are many deeply incised, steep-banked channels (some as steep as forty degrees), with outer-bank margins typified by abundant angular blocks of bank-failure material. These channels starkly contrast with the subdued topography of the Tullock Formation channels, which formed in a much moister and obviously lower energy environment bordering the Paleocene Cannonball Sea.

There is a general lack of fossil wood in the Hell Creek Formation, while the overlying Tullock Formation contains reasonably abundant wood scrap scattered throughout the channel and overbank deposits. Hell Creek fossil pollen indicates a frost-free source (Nichols et al. 1986), but we have failed to find evidence for abundant and large-scale dense vegetation. We have looked for root traces in soil horizons of the Hell Creek Formation and find only small-scale roots, not the larger roots expected for a large standing forest canopy. Such indicators, however, appear in the overlying Tullock Formation. The area was periodically dry enough during the time of Hell Creek to at least sustain wildfires like the one at the K/T boundary.

What does all of this mean? It means that Hell Creek dinosaurs were probably living in a seasonally dry environment that was subjected to flash flooding; standing tropical vegetation was probably limited to riparian habitats with well-developed interfluves of minimal crown cover (Fig. 12). In other words, at least in Montana the dinosaurs were living in a much different environment than the swamps in which we typically see them illustrated. What we see in Montana supports arguments about substantially warmer Cretaceous climates and a number of other climatic generalities that I would briefly like to discuss.

We have known for some time that the climate of high-latitude regions in the Middle and Upper Cretaceous was much warmer than it is now (Barron and Washington 1985; Lasaga, Berner, and Garrels 1985). One only need think of discoveries of dinosaurs on the northern Alaskan slope recently published by Clemens and Allison (1985) and a report by T. Rich (Society of Vertebrate Paleontology International Meetings, Rapid City, South Dakota, 1985), which place dinosaurs within a few hundred miles of the Cretaceous northern and southern

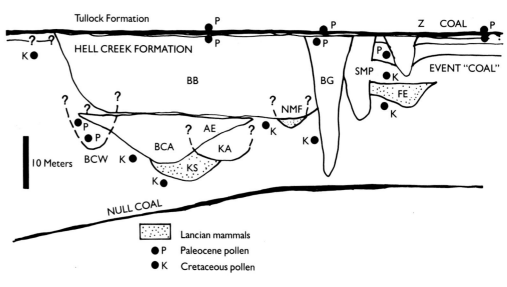

poles to be reminded that climates have changed dramatically since the Middle Cretaceous.

Climatologists and paleontologists alike tell us that high-latitude North America was hot as seen in the simplified representation of global Cretaceous temperatures (Fig. 13 herein; Barron and Washington 1985). North America was warmer by as much as fifteen to twenty-five degrees Celsius, while equatorial temperatures were warmer by only about five degrees Celsius. Geographic placement of the continents during the Middle Cretaceous can explain about five degrees Celsius, but researchers are now examining the possibility that atmospheric carbon dioxide significantly contributed to Cretaceous global warming. Climatic models recently published by Barron and Washington (1985) and Lasaga, Berner, and Garrels (1985) suggest that carbon-dioxide abundances of two to ten times current levels explain much of the remaining higher temperature. The increased abundance of carbon dioxide is further evidenced by the enormous amount of organic carbon in the form of coal and oil, which was taken out of circulation and stored in the earth's crust during Cretaceous times. This material was ultimately derived from the atmosphere and would, in turn, require much higher atmospheric carbon-dioxide concentrations than are

Figure 10. Generalized stratigraphic relationships of the Bug Creek area channel deposits with dated pollen samples shown. If vertebrate faunas are to have a significant constituent derived from reworked Cretaceous sediments, then the most ideal circumstance for such reworking would occur where a channel is eroding another channel in which the vertebrates are already concentrated. However, no such contamination was seen in any of the several opportunities presented in the diagram. Some localities (i.e., BG) cut several different faunal horizons, yet even the mammal faunas are not mixed.

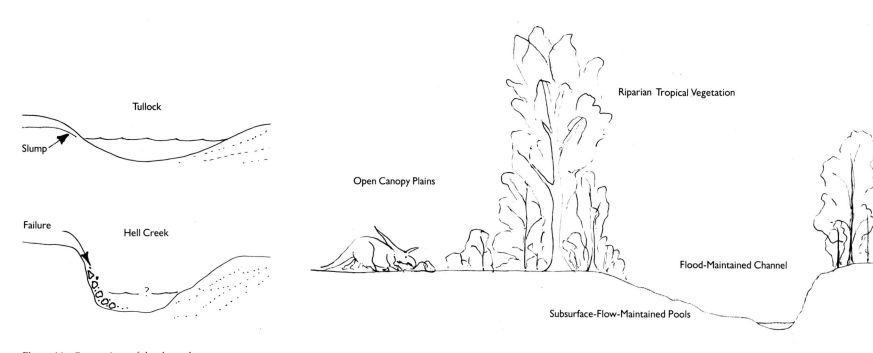

Tullock

Slump

Failure

Hell Creek

?

Open Canopy Plains

Riparian Tropical Vegetation

Flood-Maintained Channel

Subsurface-Flow-Maintained Pools

Figure 11. Comparison of the channel profiles of the Hell Creek and Tullock Formations. Tullock channel deposits are generally much larger and more extensive than those in the Hell Creek Formation and exhibit slumped channel margins. Hell Creek channel deposits are characterized by chaotic bank-failure blocks along one bank. Channels of the Tullock Formation are thought to have been flow maintained; those of the Hell Creek Formation were flood maintained.

Figure 12. Paleoenvironment of the last of the Hell Creek dinosaurs. The reconstruction shows the major elements that we can deduce from sedimentologic and fossil occurrence data.

presently observed. The climate during the Cretaceous was therefore probably much hotter than it is today and was controlled by a reasonably strong green house effect induced by carbon dioxide and perhaps methane (Fig. 14).

If the Cretaceous climate was as warm as predicted, a number of other predictions can also be made. The annual worldwide precipitation rate would have increased approximately twenty-five percent over current rates. The distribution would have been dramatically different from that seen today—the continental interiors would have been dry and subjected to flash flooding (Barron and Washington 1985), while coastal areas would have received increased precipitation, which would have sustained the abundant marsh vegetation that produced much of our Cretaceous and Paleocene coal deposits.

By using these constraints on interpretation, the paleoenvironment of the last of the dinosaurs in Montana could have looked very similar to what we see now in western Australia along the Fitzroy River: dense tropical vegetation bordering the rivers (Figs. 15, 16) with open-canopy, black soil interfluves (Fig. 17). The river channel could be expected to dry up during part of the year (Fig. 18); during these periods only deep pools, such as those in Geike Gorge (Fig. 19), would retain water by subsurface flow. Precipitation would be much more

"acid" than it is today, because of higher atmospheric carbon-dioxide concentrations, which would facilitate the leaching of soluble compounds from soils and would make them appear like wetter, present-day soils (because of the lack of calcium). In other words, the environment of the last of the dinosaurs in Montana would have looked very different from that of the tropical marsh or mature climax forest in which we see them illustrated.

The paleoenvironmental interpretation presented here—a warmer Cretaceous climate regulated by carbon dioxide and perhaps methane—introduces a host of new issues: Could the ceratopsian frill be a heat radiator or receptor rather than a defense structure? What about the head superstructures of some hadrosaurs—could they similarly be heat dissipaters or gatherers? The whole concept of climates regulated by carbon dioxide will necessitate revision of the asteroid-caused extinction hypotheses and will lead to alternative explanations for the extinction of dinosaurs as suggested by McLean (1985).

Dinosaur remains have been found in six Paleocene channel deposits in the uppermost part of the Hell Creek Formation. These remains are most probably from dinosaurs that survived the K/T boundary impact event and are found in association with mam-

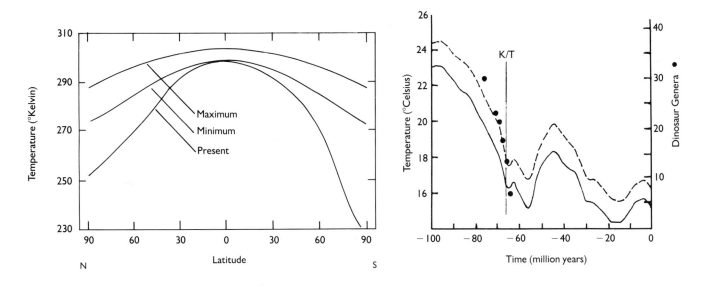

malian faunas of basal Paleocene age. Age determinations were based on fossil pollen located within the producing channel deposits and/or on stratigraphic relationships that show vertebrate-producing channel sequences truncating Paleocene beds.

These dinosaur remains are not likely to be reworked from Cretaceous bank material for a variety of reasons:

(1) The fossil vertebrates occur concentrated in clay-pebble conglomerates and are not randomly scattered throughout a channel or channel-lag deposits. Clasts, the main constituent of these conglomerates, are not likely to survive transport in excess of two kilometers, and associated vertebrates are similarly not likely to survive lengthy transport. Vertebrates do not appear in clay-silt clasts.

(2) Vertebrate abundance in overbank deposits is rare, and therefore these deposits are not likely to be a source that would produce enough fossil material to account for the abundance seen in screen-washed concentrates.

(3) Many Paleocene dinosaur remains appear unabraded with sharp and fragile surfaces intact. Such features would surely be lost through transport and reworking.

(4) Rare dinosaur taxa appear as the dominant form in some localities. If reworking had oc-

curred, certainly these faunal peculiarities would diminish.

(5) Many fossil mammals known to occur in Cretaceous deposits do not appear associated with Paleocene dinosaur remains. If reworking had occurred, it would have been necessary to selectively rework dinosaur remains while leaving other more abundant parts of the fauna behind.

Based upon presented evidence, it seems virtually certain that dinosaurs survived the K/T boundary into the Paleocene where their numbers continued to decline until local extinction occurred. The actual extinction date in the study area is difficult to determine because of a suspected unconformity at the base of the Tullock Formation. Dinosaurs were certainly extinct before the beginning of Tullock deposition in the study area.

The paleoenvironment of the last of the dinosaurs was probably quite different than currently perceived. The dinosaurs probably lived along streams with established bank vegetation and broad, open interfluves. The streams dried up periodically with only local pools retaining water by subsurface flow; these pools served to concentrate the vertebrate fauna. Flash floods were reasonably common and produced the clay-pebble conglomerate and fossil-vertebrate concentrations. The Hell Creek dinosaurs certainly were not living in lush swamps or in climax forests.

Figure 13. Worldwide mid-Cretaceous temperatures. Minimum and maximum mid-Cretaceous temperatures are compared with the present global thermoclines. Cretaceous polar regions would have been much warmer while tropical regions would have been only slightly warmer. These predictions are based upon fossil and isotope data (modified from Barron and Washington, 1985).

Figure 14. Upper Cretaceous and Paleocene dinosaur diversity compared with global temperatures over the last 100 million years. Lasaga et al. (1985) produced two curves for global temperatures; the solid line represents the best estimate, and the dashed line illustrates an alternative curve based upon a modified mean model for several variables. Dinosaur diversity was taken from Sloan et al. (1986) and scaled arbitrarily to place greatest dinosaur diversity near greatest Cretaceous temperatures during the same time period. The K/T boundary (66.4 million years ago) is shown.

Figure 15. Fitzroy River bank vegetation near the channel margin.

Figure 16. Aerial view of the Fitzroy River channel as it cuts through the Devonian reef deposits of the Canning Basin in western Australia. The environment of this region is thought to be quite similar to that of the Hell Creek Formation of Montana.

Figure 17. Open canopy on the black soil flood plain 200 meters from the Fitzroy River channel near Fitzroy Crossing, western Australia; dense riparian habitat vegetation (Fig. 16) can be seen in the background. The interfluvial environment of the last dinosaurs in Montana would have resembled that of the Fitzroy (the plain would of course have been covered with sedges rather than grasses).

Figure 18. Fitzroy River secondary channel (Billabong) showing desiccated channel floor during the dry season with the pool of Geike Gorge in the background.

Figure 19. The Geike Gorge pool of the Fitzroy River. This pool supports a variety of animals including several kinds of fish, crocodiles, and turtles and mammals in the surrounding narrow band of bank vegetation. The River ceases to flow during the dry season and is a torrent during the rainy season.

"Dawn of a New Day," by Mark Hallett. Checklist 123.

133

Acknowledgments

I wish to thank the residents of Garfield and Mc-Cone counties of Montana, especially the residents of the Nelson and Ferguson ranches and the Kountz and Sutton families of Circle, Montana, for all of the assistance provided over the last four years. A number of people have aided in the large screening operations: P. Edson, R. Ernst, M. Ferrari, R. Fowler, T. Hendrick, T. Marzolf, C. Singler, J. Smit, and W. Steig. K. Newman, J. Smit, and S. van der Kaars provided valuable palynological data. J. K. Rigby, Sr., B. Sloan, and J. Smit aided in the geologic mapping and stratigraphy. Comments by D. Archibald, B. Clemens, P. Dodson, J. Fassett, D. McClean, C. Orth, J. K. Rigby, Sr., B. Sloan, J. Smit, and N. D. Smith have been most helpful. J. K. Rigby, Sr., provided illustrations of the Fitzroy River and Geike Gorge, Western Australia. The U.S. Fish and Wildlife Service and U.S. Bureau of Land Management provided access to lands administered by them. Funding was provided by a grant to the Department of Earth Sciences by the Hill Foundation, University of Notre Dame Jesse Jones Research Fund (grant to J. K. Rigby, Jr., and Fr. R. Wasowski), and University of Notre Dame, Department of Earth Sciences Student Travel Fund.

Works Cited

Alvarez, L., W. Alvarez, F. Asaro, and H. V. Michel. 1980. Extraterrestrial cause for the Cretaceous-Tertiary extinction. *Science* 208: 1095–1108.

Alvarez, W., E. G. Kauffman, F. Surlyk, L. W. Alvarez, F. Asaro, and H. Michel. 1984. Impact theory of mass extinctions and the invertebrate fossil record. *Science* 223: 1135–41.

Archibald, J. D. 1982. *A study on Mammalia across the Cretaceous-Tertiary boundary in Garfield County, Montana.* University of California Publications in Geological Sciences 122.

Barron, E. J., and W. M. Washington. 1985. Warm Cretaceous climates: High atmospheric CO_2 and a plausible mechanism. In *The carbon cycle and atmospheric CO_2: Natural variations, Archean to Present*, ed. E. T. Sundquist and W. S. Broecker, 546–53. Geophysical Monograph 32. American Geophysical Union, Washington, D.C.

Behrensmeyer, A. K., and D. E. D. Boaz. 1980. The recent bones of Amboseli Park, Kenya in relation to east African paleoecology. In *Fossils in the making*, ed. A. K. Behrensmeyer and A. H. Hill, 72–92. Chicago: University of Chicago Press.

Bohor, B. F., E. E. Foord, P. J. Modreski, and D. M. Triplehorn. 1984. Mineralogic evidence for the impact event at the Cretaceous-Tertiary boundary. *Science* 224: 867–69.

Brookins, D. G., and J. K. Rigby, Jr. 1987. Geochronologic and geochemical study of volcanic ashes from the Kirtland Formation (Cretaceous), San Juan Basin, New Mexico. In *The Cretaceous-Tertiary boundary in the San Juan and Raton Basins, New Mexico and Colorado*, ed. J. E. Fassett and J. K. Rigby, Jr., 105–10. Special Paper 209, Geological Society of America, Boulder, Colo.

Clemens, W. A., and C. W. Allison. 1985. Late Cretaceous terrestrial vertebrate fauna, North Slope, Alaska. *Geological Society of America Abstracts with Programs* 17, no. 6: 548.

Estes, R., and P. Berberian. 1970. Paleoecology of a late Cretaceous vertebrate community from Montana. *Berviora* 343: 1–35.

Fassett, J. E. 1987. The ages of the continental upper Cretaceous Fruitland Formation and Kirtland Shale based upon a projection of ammonite zones from the Lewis Shale, San Juan Basin, New Mexico and Colorado. In *The Cretaceous-Tertiary boundary in the San Juan and Raton Basins, New Mexico and Colorado*, ed. J. E. Fassett and J. K. Rigby, Jr., 5–16. Special Paper 209, Geological Society of America, Boulder, Colo.

Fassett, J. E., and J. K. Rigby, Jr., eds. 1987. *The Cretaceous-Tertiary boundary in the San Juan and*

Raton Basins, New Mexico and Colorado. Special Paper 209, Geological Society of America, Boulder, Colo.

Lasaga, A. C., R. A. Berner, and R. M. Garrels. 1985. An improved geochemical model of atmospheric CO_2 fluctuations over the past one hundred million years. In *The carbon cycle and atmospheric CO_2: Natural variations, Archean to Present,* ed. E. T. Sundquist and W. S. Broecker, 397–411. Geophysical Monograph 32, American Geophysical Union, Washington, D.C.

Leopold, L. B., and T. Maddock, Jr. 1953. *The hydrolic geometry of stream channels and some physiographic implications.* U.S. Geological Society Professional Paper 252.

Lupton, C., D. Gabriel, and R. M. West. 1980. Paleobiology and depositional setting of a late Cretaceous vertebrate locality, Hell Creek Formation, McCone County, Montana. *Contributions in Geology, University of Wyoming* 18: 117–26.

McKenna, M. C. 1965. Collecting microvertebrate fossils by washing and screening. In *Handbook of paleontological techniques,* ed. B. Kummel and D. Raup, 193–203. San Francisco: Freeman.

McLean, D. M. 1985. Mantle degassing induced the dead ocean in the Cretaceous-Tertiary transition. In *The carbon cycle and atmospheric CO_2: Natural variations, Archean to Present,* ed. E. T. Sundquist and W. S. Broecker, 493–503. Geophysical Monograph 32. American Geophysical Union, Washington, D.C.

Newman, K. R. 1987. Biostratigraphic correlation of Cretaceous-Tertiary boundary rocks, Colorado to San Juan Basin, New Mexico. In *The Cretaceous-Tertiary boundary in the San Juan and Raton Basins, New Mexico and Colorado,* ed. J. E. Fassett and J. K. Rigby, Jr., 151–64. Special Paper 209, Geological Society of America, Boulder, Colo.

Nichols, D. J., D. M. Jarzen, C. J. Orth, and P. Q. Oliver. 1986. Palynological and iridium anomalies at Cretaceous-Tertiary boundary, south-central Saskatchewan. *Science* 231: 714–17.

Orth, C. J., J. S. Gilmore, J. D. Knight, C. L. Pillmore, R. H. Tschudy, and J. E. Fassett. 1981. An iridium abundance anomaly at the palynological Cretaceous-Tertiary Boundary in northern New Mexico. *Science* 214: 1341–43.

———. 1982. Iridium abundance measurements across the Cretaceous-Tertiary Boundary in the San Juan and Raton Basins of northern New Mexico. In *Geological implications of impacts of large asteroids and comets on the Earth,* ed. L. T. Silver and P. H. Schulz, 423–33. Special Paper 190, Geological Society of America, Boulder, Colo.

Rigby, J. K., Jr. 1985. Paleocene dinosaurs: The reworked sample question. *Geological Society of America Abstracts with Programs* 17, no. 4: 262.

Rigby, J. K., Jr., and R. E. Sloan. 1985. Dinosaur decline and eventual extinction near the Cretaceous-Tertiary boundary, Hell Creek Fm., MT. *Geological Society of America Abstracts with Programs* 17, no. 6: 7009.

Rigby, J. K., Jr., and D. Wolberg. 1987. The therian mammalian fauna (Campanian) of quarry 1, Fossil Forest study area, San Juan Basin, New Mexico. In *The Cretaceous-Tertiary boundary in the San Juan and Raton Basins, New Mexico and Colorado,* ed. J. E. Fassett and J. K. Rigby, Jr., 51–79. Special Paper 209, Geological Society of America, Boulder, Colo.

Rigby, J. K., Jr., K. Newman, J. Smit, R. E. Sloan, J. K. Rigby, Sr., and S. van der Kaars. Paleocene dinosaurs from the Hell Creek Formation, McCone County, Montana. *Palaios,* in press.

Sloan, R. E., and L. Van Valen. 1965. Cretaceous mammals from Montana. *Science* 148: 220–27.

Sloan, R. E., J. K. Rigby, Jr., L. Van Valen, and D. Gabriel. 1986. Gradual extinction of dinosaurs and the simultaneous radiation of ungulate mammals in the Hell Creek Formation of McCone County, Montana. *Science* 232: 629–33.

Smit, J., and G. Klaver. 1981. Sanidine spherules at the Cretaceous/Tertiary boundary indicate a large impact event. *Nature* 292: 47–49.

Smith, N. D. 1972. Flume experiments on the durability of mud clasts. *Journal of Sedimentary Petrology* 42, no. 2: 378–83.

Tschudy, R. H., C. L. Pillmore, C. J. Orth, J. S. Gilmore, and J. D. Knight. 1984. Disruption of the terrigenous plant ecosystem after the Cretaceous-Tertiary boundary, western interior. *Science* 225: 1030–32.

Wolbach, W. S., R. S. Lewis, and E. Anders. 1985. Cretaceous extinction: Evidence for wild fires and search for meteoritic material. *Science* 230: 167–70.

APPENDIX

Simplified Classification of the Reptiles Listing the Major Groups of Dinosaurs

CLASS REPTILIA

Subclass Anapsida (Tortoises, turtles, and their extinct relatives)

Subclass Lepidosauria (Lizards, snakes, and their extinct relatives)

SUBCLASS ARCHOSAURIA

    Order Thecodontia (Thecodonts, all extinct)†

    Order Crocodilia (Crocodiles and their extinct relatives)†

    Order Pterosauria (Flying reptiles, all extinct)†

    ORDER SAURISCHIA (Lizard-hipped dinosaurs)*

        SUBORDER THEROPODA (Carnivorous dinosaurs, e.g., *Tyrannosaurus*)*

        SUBORDER SAUROPODOMORPHA (Giant dinosaurs, e.g., *Diplodocus*)*

    ORDER ORNITHISCHIA (Bird-hipped dinosaurs)*

        SUBORDER ORNITHOPODA ("duck-billed" dinosaurs, e.g., *Corythodon*)*

        SUBORDER STEGOSAURIA (dinosaurs protected by plates and spines, e.g., *Stegosaurus*)

        SUBORDER ANKYLOSAURIA (other armored dinosaurs, e.g., *Ankylosaurus*)*

        SUBORDER CERATOPSIA (Horned dinosaurs, e.g., *Triceratops*)*

Subclass Euryapsida (includes marine plesiosaurs, all extinct)

Subclass Ichthyopterygia (includes marine ichthyosaurs, all extinct)

Subclass Synapsida (includes mammallike reptiles, all extinct)

*Dinosaurs
†Other reptiles discussed in this volume.

Appendix illustrations by Mark Hallett
©Mark Hallet, 1987

Theropods

Theropods were bipedal, flesh-eating dinosaurs with sharp teeth. Many had grasping fore limbs, and in some these fore limbs were tiny with three, or sometimes only two, fingers. Two groups of theropods are recognized: the smaller coelurosaurs and larger carnosaurs. Both are known from the Triassic period, but only carnosaurs persisted to the end of the Cretaceous period.

Dilophosaurus

Acrocanthosaurus

Deinonych[us]

Gallimimus

Segnosaurus

Herrerasaurus

Plateosaurus

Riojasaurus

Prosauropods

The suborder Sauropodomorpha contains two groups of dinosaurs: the prosauropods and sauropods. Prosauropods, of which the 6-meter-long *Plateosaurus* is typical, were primitive, partially bipedal Triassic forms. Some were of considerable size, but all were smaller than their sauropod descendants.

Camarasaurus

Mamenchisaurus

Saltasaurus

Oviraptor

Tarbosaurus

Archaeopteryx

Coelophysis

Ohmdenosaurus

Ceratosaurus

Brachiosaurus

Sauropods

Giants in an age of giant reptiles, sauropods included the longest, heaviest, and tallest land animals ever to have lived and were prominent components of Jurassic and Cretaceous faunas. Although all were quadrupedal, some sauropods may have reared up on their hind legs to browse from tall trees. At one time depicted as snorkeling water dwellers, sauropods probably spent much of their time on land. One family, the titanosaurids, evolved armored scutes along the back that are thought to have provided protection from predators.

Stegosaurs

These dinosaurs were characterized by bony plates on their backs and spiked tails. Blood vessels in the skin overlying the plates could have dissipated excess heat from the body and perhaps the orientation of the plates may have lowered the body temperature by channeling air over their skin. Stegosaurs had mosaics of bony nodules in their skin that, together with the spikes on their tail, may have offered some protection against predators.

Ceratopsians

The ceratopsians had parrotlike beaks for cropping tough vegetation and a backwardly projecting head shield that protected the neck. Known only from the Cretaceous, the different ceratopsian genera may be distinguished by the number and development of horns that were variously located on the nose, brow, and neck shield. Although primarily defensive weapons, the horns might also have been used in territorial or mating contests.

Ankylosaurs

The Ankylosauria were the most heavily armored Cretaceous dinosaurs and comprised two distinct groups. The nodosaurs had short bodies and long tails with their neck, back, and tail protected by flat or keeled plates; some had spines projecting from the neck. The ankylosaurs had long, low bodies protected by keeled and conical plates; ankylosaurs lacked spines but had short tails that ended in bony clubs.

Euoplocephalus

Saichania

Hylaeosaurus

Pachyrhinosaurus

Protoceratops

CONTENTS OF VOLUME I

INDEX

Compiled by Roberta Goodwin.
Boldface numerals indicate illustrations.

"Australian Dinosaurs." © Mark Hallett.

"Australian Dinosaurs." © Mark Hallett.

Stegosaurus stenops, by Stephen Czerkas.
Checklist 144.

147

PHOTOGRAPHERS

Lenders to the exhibition and the following organizations supplied photographs for reproduction in this volume.

American Museum of Natural History, Department of Library Services: pages viii–ix and 87 (right, Transparency No. 2441).

Kevin Aulenback: page 107, center.

Steve Jackson: pages x, xi, 53, 56, 57, 59, 61, 62.

Natural History Museum of Los Angeles County, Photography Division: pages vi–vii, xii, 6, 23, 26, 27, 30–31, 39, 100, 104, 105, 108, 109, 112, 118, 133.

J. Keith Rigby, Sr.: page 132.

Smithsonian Institution (Photo numbers in parentheses): pages 82 (28531), 84 (top, 24561; center, 29463; bottom, 24562), 85 (24563), 86 (left, 25351), 87 (left, 24564), 88 (left, 14401; right, 26450), 89 (26444), 91, 92 (29899), 93 (top), 94 (top, 24559), 95 (top left, 26445; top right, 28531).

Veronica Tagland: pages i–iii, 136–141,

Daspletosaurus, by Eleanor Kish. Courtesy National Museum of Natural Sciences, National Museums of Canada.

Project management by ROBIN A. SIMPSON
Copyediting by KATHLEEN PRECIADO
Designed by DANA LEVY, Perpetua Press, Los Angeles
Production Coordination by LETITIA BURNS O'CONNOR
Typeset in Sabon and Gill Sans by WILSTED & TAYLOR, Oakland
Printed by DAI NIPPON PRINTING CO, Japan